MASSACHUSETTS TEST PREP

Reading and Writing

Common Core Workbook

Grade 6

ISBN 978-1507836972

CONTENTS

INTRODUCTION
For Parents, Teachers, and Tutors

Developing Common Core Reading and Writing Skills

The state of Massachusetts has adopted the Common Core State Standards. These standards describe what students are expected to know. Students will be instructed based on these standards and the PARCC assessments will include questions based on these standards. This workbook will develop the Common Core reading and writing skills that students are expected to have, while preparing students for the state tests and giving students practice completing a range of reading and writing tasks. The emphasis in this workbook is on writing skills, but complementary reading skills are also covered as students complete tasks involving providing written answers to reading comprehension questions.

Completing Practice Sets

This workbook is divided into 10 practice sets. Each practice set includes four tasks that progress from simple to more complex. The types of tasks are described below.

Task Type	Details
Short Passage with Questions	These tasks contain a short passage followed by reading comprehension questions requiring written answers. They also include a Core Writing Skills Practice exercise that focuses on one key writing skill. These exercises may require students to respond to a text, complete a research project, or complete a writing task.
Long Passage with Essay Question	These tasks contain a long passage followed by an essay question requiring a written answer of 1 to 2 pages. They also include hints and planning guidance to help students develop effective writing skills.
Personal Narrative Writing Task	These tasks contain a writing prompt for a personal narrative, as well as hints and planning guidance.
Short Story Writing Task	These tasks contain a writing prompt for a story, as well as hints and planning guidance.
Argument Writing Task	These tasks contain a writing prompt for an argument, as well as hints and planning guidance.
Explanatory Writing Task	These tasks contain a writing prompt for an essay, as well as hints and planning guidance.

By completing the practice sets, students will have experience with all types of Common Core writing tasks. This includes writing in response to passages, writing all the types of texts covered in the Common Core standards, gathering information from sources, and completing research projects.

Some of the writing tasks also include guides for editing and revising completed work. This encourages students to review their work and improve on it, while the checklists help ensure that students focus on the key criteria that work is judged on. This will help prepare students for the writing tasks found on assessments, as well as guide students on the key features of strong student writing.

Preparing for the PARCC English Language Arts/Literacy Assessments

Students will be assessed each year by taking a set of tests known as the PARCC assessments. The PARCC assessments will be more rigorous than past tests, will involve more writing tasks, will focus more strongly on analyzing text closely and using evidence from text, will require students to complete more complex tasks, and will have a stronger emphasis on higher-order thinking skills like analyzing, evaluating, or making connections.

This workbook will help prepare students for the PARCC assessments. The questions and exercises will develop the more advanced Common Core skills, give students ongoing practice with more rigorous questions, provide extensive experience providing written answers, help students write effective essays and narratives, and help develop higher-order thinking skills. This will ensure that students have the skills and experience they need to perform well on the PARCC assessments.

Reading and Writing

Practice Set 1

This practice set contains four writing tasks. These are described below.

Task 1: Short Passage with Questions

This task has a short passage followed by questions. Read each question carefully. Then write your answer in the space provided.

You can also practice writing skills by completing the Core Writing Skills Practice exercise.

Task 2: Short Passage with Questions

This task has a short passage followed by questions. Read each question carefully. Then write your answer in the space provided.

You can also practice writing skills by completing the Core Writing Skills Practice exercise.

Task 3: Long Passage with Essay Question

This task has a longer passage with an essay question. Read the passage, complete the planning page, and then write or type your answer.

Task 4: Personal Narrative Writing Task

This final task requires you to write a personal narrative. Read the writing prompt, complete the planning page, and then write or type your answer.

Task 1: Short Passage with Questions

Scorpion and Frog

Once upon a time, a scorpion was walking along a river bank. He was journeying north to find a log that he could use to cross to the other side. On his way, the scorpion saw a frog swimming by.

"Would you be so kind as to carry me across the river?" the scorpion called out.

His question was met with silence, as the frog looked upon him with a distrustful expression.

"My friend, I assure you that I will not sting you! For if I do, you will sink and I too shall drown," the scorpion said.

The frog thought for a moment and then nodded, moving closer to the river bank. The scorpion walked onto the frog's back and they began to make their way across the river. Halfway across the river, the frog felt a stinger lunge into its back. The frog began to feel weak and sank slowly into the current. The frog looked up at the scorpion.

"Why did you do that? Now you too will die!" the frog said.

"I am sorry my new friend," the scorpion said. "I am a scorpion. It's my nature."

CORE WRITING SKILLS PRACTICE

Describe how the scorpion convinces the frog to trust him.

_____

_____

_____

_____

---

1   Describe **three** ways that you can tell that the passage is a fable.

    1: _____

    _____

    2: _____

    _____

    3: _____

    _____

2   What is the theme of the passage?

Hint   The theme of a passage is the idea it expresses, or a lesson it aims to teach. Think about what lesson the frog learns.

_____

_____

_____

_____

_____

Task 2: Short Passage with Questions

The Exam

March 6

Dear Annie,

I hope you are well. I'm a little worried about how I am going in math class. I can do the geometry pretty easily. For some reason, shapes just make sense to me. But a lot of the algebra problems just look like strings of numbers, symbols, and funky letters. It's like a tapestry of symbols that my brain just can't understand.

As you know, my brother Kevin is quite a whiz at math. I asked him for some help, but he's not very good at explaining things simply. In fact, he really just confused me even more! Mom is going to help me study and is also going to ask if Miss Bert will help tutor me during lunch tomorrow. That would definitely be helpful. I really hope I can figure this out soon. It's getting really stressful and I really want to do better.

Bye for now,

Alex

CORE WRITING SKILLS PRACTICE
WRITE A PERSUASIVE LETTER

Imagine that you are Annie and have just received Alex's letter. You want to write back to Alex and make her feel better about her math class. You might want to give Alex some study tips, help her relax, or just encourage her to keep trying. Write a letter to Alex giving her some advice.

1   Complete the web with **three** things that Alex does to try to learn algebra.

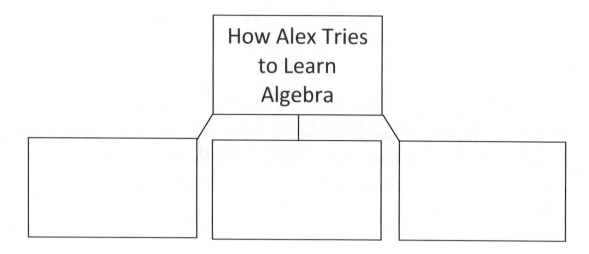

2   Alex describes Kevin as being "quite a whiz at math." What does Alex mean by this?

Hint   Focus on what the word *whiz* describes about Kevin. In your answer, describe what the word *whiz* shows about Kevin.

_____

_____

_____

_____

_____

Task 3: Long Passage with Essay Question

Directions: Read the passage below. Then answer the question that follows. Use the planning page to plan your writing. Then write or type your essay.

Changing a Light Bulb

Changing a light bulb is a common task in most households. Light bulbs operate on different voltages and may be clipped or screwed into position. You should always ensure that you have spare light bulbs that are suitable in your possession. When a bulb fails and the light goes out, you should first make sure that the switch is placed in the off position. Then find an alternative source of light so you can adequately see in the darkened room.

To change a ceiling bulb you may need to climb a step ladder or stand on a secured chair. It is very important that this equipment is reliable and safe before you climb it. Take a new bulb and remove it from its packaging. Take care to ensure that the old bulb is not too hot before you remove it from the light fitting. Once the old bulb is removed, place it safely to the side or put it back in the new bulb's box. It is also a good idea to check that the replacement bulb has the same size and shape fitting as the original bulb. This is a good final check to make sure you are not about to try and fit the wrong type of bulb. Once you are sure that the new bulb is correct, attach the new bulb to the fitting. If it is clipped into place, then make sure that it is gripped tightly in place after fitting. Similarly, ensure that it is firmly in position if you are required to screw it in place.

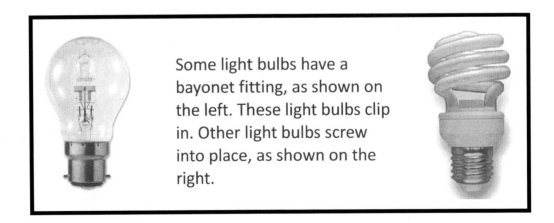

Some light bulbs have a bayonet fitting, as shown on the left. These light bulbs clip in. Other light bulbs screw into place, as shown on the right.

Once the light bulb is secure, you can leave the fitting and perform a test. Switch the light on and check that its glow is both bright and consistent. Although it is very rare, a new bulb that is faulty or fitted incorrectly can shatter. Be sure to stand back from the light when switching it on. It is also important not to stare directly at the light as this can cause damage to the eyes.

Discard the old bulb and packaging safely and responsibly. Be sure to keep all of your bulbs in a safe location and out of the reach of infants.

1   There are several dangers that need to be avoided when changing a light bulb. Describe **three** problems that can occur when changing a light bulb and explain how each problem can be prevented.

In your answer, be sure to
- describe **three** problems that can occur when changing a light bulb
- explain how each problem can be prevented
- use details from the passage
- write an answer of between 1 and 2 pages

Hint

The question tells you to describe three problems that can occur. When a question tells you to write about a certain number of items, be sure to follow it. You will not get extra marks for describing more problems that can occur! Instead, focus on clearly describing three problems and explaining how to prevent the problems.

You should use details from the passage in your answer, but you can also use your own ideas. For example, the passage states that the ladder used should be safe. You could use this information and describe how the ladder should be checked to prevent a fall. But you could also include your own suggestions, such as having another person with you to help keep you steady. Adding your own ideas to your answer will make your work stand out from the rest.

Planning Page

Summary

Write a brief summary of what you are going to write about.

Supporting Details

Write down the facts, details, or examples you are going to include in your answer.

Outline

Write a plan for what you are going to write. Include the main points you want to cover and the order you will cover them.

Task 4: Personal Narrative Writing Task

Directions: Read the writing prompt below. Use the planning page to plan your writing. Then write or type your answer.

Sometimes people can inspire you. Think about a time when someone inspired you. It could be someone you know, someone you have read about, or someone from a book or movie.

Write a composition describing a time when someone inspired you. Explain who the person was, what the person did, and how the person inspired you.

Hint

Make sure you answer each part of the question. Remember that you need to include the following:

- who inspired you
- what the person did to inspire you
- how the person inspired you

When you write your outline, make sure that it covers all of the parts of the question.

Planning Page

Summary

Write a brief summary of what you are going to write about.

Outline

Write a plan for what you are going to write. Include the main points you want to cover and the order you will cover them.

Writing and Editing Checklist

After you finish writing your personal narrative, you can use this guide to review and edit your work. Use the questions as a guide to finding ways you can improve your work.

Writing Checklist

- ✓ Does your work have a strong opening? Does it introduce the main ideas or set the scene well?
- ✓ Is your work well-organized? Is related information grouped together? Does each paragraph have one main idea?
- ✓ Does your work have an effective ending? Does it tie up the events well?
- ✓ Is your work focused? Are there any details that do not fit with your main ideas?
- ✓ Do your ideas flow well? Have you used words and phrases to link ideas well?
- ✓ Have you used strong words? Are there words that could be replaced with better ones?
- ✓ Have you used effective descriptions? Could your descriptions be improved?
- ✓ Have you used sensory details? Could you add more sensory details to help readers imagine the scene?

Editing Checklist

- ✓ Have you used a variety of sentence structures? Are your sentences all written correctly?
- ✓ Is the grammar correct?
- ✓ Are all words spelled correctly? You can check the spelling of any words you are not sure of.
- ✓ Is punctuation used correctly?
- ✓ If dialogue is used, is it punctuated correctly?
- ✓ Are all words capitalized correctly?

Reading and Writing

Practice Set 2

This practice set contains four writing tasks. These are described below.

Task 1: Short Passage with Questions

This task has a short passage followed by questions. Read each question carefully. Then write your answer in the space provided.

You can also practice writing skills by completing the Core Writing Skills Practice exercise.

Task 2: Short Passage with Questions

This task has a short passage followed by questions. Read each question carefully. Then write your answer in the space provided.

You can also practice writing skills by completing the Core Writing Skills Practice exercise.

Task 3: Short Story Writing Task

This task requires you to write a short story. Read the writing prompt, complete the planning page, and then write or type your answer.

Task 4: Argument Writing Task

This final task requires you to write an argument. Read the writing prompt, complete the planning page, and then write or type your answer.

Task 1: Short Passage with Questions

Doyle Brunson

Affectionately known as "Big Poppa" or "Texas Dolly," Doyle Brunson is one of the most respected professional card players in the world. He is easily recognized in his trademark cowboy hat. He has been playing cards professionally for over 50 years.

Brunson was born in 1933 in Fisher County, Texas. He is one of only three players ever to win back to back main event titles at the World Series of Poker. He won these titles in 1976 and 1977. He has gone on to achieve many other great things, but nothing quite as amazing as this pair of championship wins.

©Wikimedia Commons

The two wins of 1976 and 1977 have gone down in history for another reason. Each time he won, Brunson was holding the same two cards in the final hand. They were a ten and a two. It was a coincidence that stunned everybody at the time, and is still remembered today. In fact, this hand is now known by card players everywhere as "The Brunson."

CORE WRITING SKILLS PRACTICE
WRITE A RESEARCH REPORT

This passage is a biography of Doyle Brunson. Choose one famous American from the list below. Research and write a short biography of that person.

Clara Barton
Henry Ford
Venus Williams
Louis Armstrong
Babe Ruth
Helen Keller

---

1   Describe **two** facts and **two** opinions given about Doyle Brunson.

Fact 1: _____

_____

Fact 2: _____

_____

Opinion 1: _____

_____

Opinion 2: _____

_____

2   Describe **two** reasons Brunson's wins in 1976 and 1977 were special.

_____

_____

_____

_____

_____

_____

Task 2: Short Passage with Questions

Food Poisoning

Bacteria grow quickly in the right conditions. When food isn't prepared, kept, or handled properly it has the potential to make you very ill. Food poisoning occurs when bacteria are introduced into food before it is eaten. Luckily, it is quite easy to prevent food poisoning. All you have to do is follow a few simple rules.

1: Wash your hands and the equipment you're going to use to prepare and serve the food.

2: Don't use the same chopping board for chopping meat that you use to prepare fruit and vegetables.

3: Ensure your food is cooked thoroughly. The cooking process destroys most harmful bacteria, so this step can prevent food poisoning even when the raw food contains bacteria.

4: Make sure your refrigerator temperature is set low enough.

5: Follow the directions on packaging for how to store foods once they are open, and for how long to store food for.

6: Don't unfreeze and then refreeze food.

CORE WRITING SKILLS PRACTICE

Step 6 includes the words *unfreeze* and *refreeze*. Write a definition of each word based on the prefixes. Then list **three** more examples of base words that can have both the prefixes *un-* and *re-* added to them.

unfreeze: _____

refreeze: _____

1. _____   2. _____   3. _____

---

1   What is the cause of food poisoning?

Hint

This question is asking you to summarize specific information given in the passage. Make sure you use your own words when writing your answer.

_____

_____

_____

_____

2   Why do you think it is important not to use the same chopping board for meat that you use for fruit and vegetables?

Hint

Think about how the cause of food poisoning relates to this rule.

_____

_____

_____

_____

Task 3: Short Story Writing Task

Directions: Read the writing prompt below. Use the planning page to plan your writing. Then write or type your answer.

"Just close your eyes, count to ten, and when you wake up you will be on the surface of the planet Europa," the captain said. As Greg closed his eyes, he imagined what Europa might be like.

Write a story about what happens when Greg arrives on the planet Europa.

Hint

The writing prompt tells you that your story should be about Greg's arrival on Europa. Use this as the starting point and think of a story based around this idea. Your writing should not just describe the planet, but should describe some events that occur once Greg arrives.

A good way to approach this story is to think of a problem that occurs when Greg arrives. The start of the story will describe the problem. The middle of the story will describe Greg facing the problem or trying to solve it. The end of the story will describe Greg solving it. By approaching the writing task this way, you will end up with a focused story based around a series of events.

Planning Page

The Story
Write a summary of your story.

The Beginning
Describe what is going to happen at the start of your story.

The Middle
Describe what is going to happen in the middle of your story.

The End
Describe what is going to happen at the end of your story.

Task 4: Argument Writing Task

Directions: Read the writing prompt below. Use the planning page to plan your writing. Then write or type your answer.

Your school band has been invited to play at a major sporting event. The school band considers it an honor, but does not have the money to go. Imagine that you want to encourage people to consider donating money so the band can go.

Write a letter to your school newsletter encouraging people to donate to the cause. Use reasons, facts, and/or examples to encourage people to support the school band.

Hint

The writing prompt describes the purpose of your writing. In this case, you want to persuade people to support the school band. You will need to give reasons that will convince people that it is important that the school band plays at the sporting event. Think of 2 or 3 good reasons to use in your letter.

Planning Page

Summary
Write a brief summary of your claim.

Supporting Details
Write down the facts, details, or examples you are going to include.

Outline
Write a plan for what you are going to write. Include the main points you want to cover and the order you will cover them.

Writing and Editing Checklist

After you finish writing your argument, you can use this guide to review and edit your work. Use the questions as a guide to finding ways you can improve your work.

Writing Checklist

✓ Does your work have one clear claim?
✓ Does your work have a strong opening? Does the opening introduce the topic and state the claim?
✓ Is your claim supported? Have you used clear reasons to support your claim?
✓ Have you used enough evidence? Is your evidence all relevant?
✓ Is your work well-organized? Is related information grouped together? Does each paragraph have one main idea?
✓ Do your ideas flow well? Have you used words and phrases to link ideas well?
✓ Does your work have a strong ending? Does the ending restate the main idea and tie up the argument?

Editing Checklist

✓ Have you used a variety of sentence structures? Are your sentences all written correctly?
✓ Is the grammar correct?
✓ Are all words spelled correctly? You can check the spelling of any words you are not sure of.
✓ Is punctuation used correctly?
✓ Are all words capitalized correctly?

Reading and Writing

Practice Set 3

This practice set contains four writing tasks. These are described below.

Task 1: Short Passage with Questions

This task has a short passage followed by questions. Read each question carefully. Then write your answer in the space provided.

You can also practice writing skills by completing the Core Writing Skills Practice exercise.

Task 2: Short Passage with Questions

This task has a short passage followed by questions. Read each question carefully. Then write your answer in the space provided.

You can also practice writing skills by completing the Core Writing Skills Practice exercise.

Task 3: Long Passage with Essay Question

This task has a longer passage with an essay question. Read the passage, complete the planning page, and then write or type your answer.

Task 4: Explanatory Writing Task

This final task requires you to write an essay that explains something. Read the writing prompt, complete the planning page, and then write or type your answer.

Task 1: Short Passage with Questions

Bless You

Sneezing is a bodily reflex similar to a cough. It serves the same purpose of a cough, which is to remove foreign bodies and irritants from the body.

The scientific term for sneezing is sternutation. There are four main reasons that people sneeze.

- Irritation – people sneeze when something irritates the nose
- Light – people can sneeze when they are suddenly exposed to bright light
- Feeling full – some people have a rare condition where they sneeze as a response to feeling very full after a meal
- Infection – many infections by viruses, including the common cold, can cause people to sneeze

The most common reason people sneeze is due to irritation. Many people sneeze when they breathe in dust, pollen, or other irritants in the air. This condition is known as hay fever, and is most common in spring when there is pollen in the air.

CORE WRITING SKILLS PRACTICE

There are simple steps that people can take to prevent hay fever. Use the Internet to research how hay fever can be prevented and list three ways below.

1. _____

_____

2. _____

_____

3. _____

_____

---

1   What do you think is the least common cause of sneezing? Explain your
    answer.

Hint   This question is asking you to make an inference based on the passage. Make sure you explain how you decided what the least common cause of sneezing is.

_____

_____

_____

_____

_____

_____

2   Which detail from the passage did you find most interesting or surprising?
    Explain why you found that detail interesting or surprising.

_____

_____

_____

_____

_____

_____

Task 2: Short Passage with Questions

The Cookie Thief

Max was sitting at his desk early one morning flipping wildly through the pages of his notebook and pinning up hastily written notes on his corkboard. Max had covered his entire corkboard with clues, and drawn maps of his house. He paced back and forth, stared at the board, and then remembered something else. He scribbled something on another piece of note paper and added it to the board.

"I'm going to find out who ate my cookies if it's the last thing I do!" Max said as he worked away on his investigation. Max's dog Lucky just stared up at him.

Max jumped up and headed for his sister's room. Along with his father, she was the main suspect. Before he had even set foot outside of his room, Max tripped on something, stumbled, and fell. Max sat up and shook himself off. He looked around to see what he had tripped on. Right in front of him was a plastic bowl filled with cookie crumbs. Max suddenly remembered that he'd snuck out in the middle of the night for a snack. He was suddenly glad that he hadn't stormed in and blamed his sister.

CORE WRITING SKILLS PRACTICE

Imagine that Max had stormed in and blamed his sister for eating the cookies. Write a paragraph describing the argument Max and his sister might have had.

_____

_____

_____

_____

_____

---

1   Who was the cookie thief? How does Max find out who the cookie thief was?

_____

_____

_____

_____

_____

2   Identify the hyperbole used in the passage and explain why the author included it.

Hint   Hyperbole is a literary technique where exaggeration is used to make a point or emphasize the qualities of something.

_____

_____

_____

_____

3 How does the author create a sense of urgency in the passage? Use details from the passage in your answer.

Hint Focus on the words and phrases the author uses to describe Max and what he is doing. List these words and phrases in your answer and explain their impact.

_____

_____

_____

_____

_____

_____

_____

_____

_____

_____

_____

_____

Writing and Editing Checklist

After you finish writing your answer to question 3, you can use this guide to review and edit your work. Use the questions as a guide to finding ways you can improve your work.

Writing Checklist

- ✓ Does your work have a strong opening? Does it introduce the topic and the main ideas?
- ✓ Is your work well-organized? Is related information grouped together? Does each paragraph have one main idea?
- ✓ Have you clearly explained how the author creates a sense of urgency? Have you used examples from the passage to support your answer?
- ✓ Is your work focused? Are there any details that do not fit with your main ideas?
- ✓ Do your ideas flow well? Have you used words and phrases to link ideas well?

Editing Checklist

- ✓ Have you used a variety of sentence structures? Are your sentences all written correctly?
- ✓ Is the grammar correct?
- ✓ Are all words spelled correctly? You can check the spelling of any words you are not sure of.
- ✓ Is punctuation used correctly?
- ✓ If dialogue is used, is it punctuated correctly?
- ✓ Are all words capitalized correctly?

Task 3: Long Passage with Essay Question

Directions: Read the passage below. Then answer the question that follows. Use the planning page to plan your writing. Then write or type your essay.

Elvis Presley

Elvis Presley was an American singer and actor who became one of the most popular performers of the twentieth century. Born in Tennessee in 1935, he began his pop career in 1954 at the age of 19. At this time, he was signed as a performer by Sun Records. The label's owner, Sam Phillips, believed that Presley had the talent to reach a wider American audience than any other performer of the time. Presley's upbeat tempo and energized performances were the building blocks of his early career and helped make him an icon.

His first single was titled "Heartbreak Hotel" and was released in January of 1956. It went straight to number one in the billboard charts. His sound was classified as rock and roll and a brand new era of music was born. He continued to achieve astonishing success with a string of number one singles over the next few years. This was despite some controversy surrounding his uninhibited and excitable performances. His talent was such that no amount of criticism could stop him. He even made his Hollywood film debut in the movie *Love Me Tender* in 1956.

Being conscripted into the military in 1958 did halt his progress for two years. In 1960, he managed to return and was soon producing his best and most commercially successful work. As the decade progressed, he reduced his level of live performances and tours. Instead, he focused on appearing in blockbuster Hollywood movies and recording their soundtrack albums. Although some of his work at this time was disregarded by critics, he became even more popular with his fans.

In 1968, Elvis returned to the stage. He performed a comeback special on television and then performed a series of tours and Las Vegas concerts. In 1973, he performed the first live concert that was broadcast to a global television audience. This was called *Aloha from Hawaii* and was viewed by an estimated 1.5 billion people. This was to be one of the crowning achievements of his varied and award winning career. The following four years saw his health suffer a dramatic decline. Shortly after, he met a sudden and tragic death in 1977, aged just 42.

His later years saw him gain a large amount of weight and develop an addiction to prescription drugs. It was this inevitable strain on his body that ultimately cost him his life. His musical talent and acting ability saw him win three Grammy Awards and also their lifetime achievement award at the age of 36. He has also had the honor of being inducted into four separate music halls of fame. Elvis stands alone as the most influential cultural music icon for the twentieth century and his music is still remembered fondly today.

1   Elvis Presley's life can be described as one full of great achievements and great struggles. Write an essay in which you describe the achievements and struggles of his life. Use details from the passage to support your answer.

In your answer, be sure to
- describe Elvis Presley's achievements
- describe Elvis Presley's struggles
- include details from the passage
- write an answer of between 1 and 2 pages

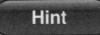

Hint

An essay that scores full points will go beyond just restating information from the passage. Instead, use the information to make a strong argument about Elvis Presley. This will show that you are thinking about what you are reading and forming your own opinion.

In this case, a good argument would be that Elvis Presley's story is sad. This could be supported by describing his major achievements and by describing how his struggles caused him to lose his life at a young age. This essay would answer the question, but also shows insight into the topic.

Planning Page

Summary

Write a brief summary of what you are going to write about.

Supporting Details

Write down the facts, details, or examples you are going to include in your answer.

Outline

Write a plan for what you are going to write. Include the main points you want to cover and the order you will cover them.

Task 4: Explanatory Writing Task

Directions: Read the writing prompt below. Use the planning page to plan your writing. Then write or type your answer.

Technologies like television, computers, mobile phones, and the Internet are important parts of many people's lives today. Think about how you use technology in your life.

Write an essay describing what type of technology is most important to you. In your essay, explain how you use that type of technology in your life.

Hint

Stay focused! You might be able to think of many different technologies you could write about, but don't try to write about them all. Instead, choose just one technology and focus on writing an essay describing why that technology is important to you and what you use it for.

If you can, try to think of a specific example where that technology was very helpful to you. For example, imagine that you want to write about how your mobile phone makes you feel safe because there is always someone to call. A strong essay would make this statement and then describe an example of where you called someone for help. Good essays often feature specific examples of real situations.

Planning Page

Summary

Write a brief summary of what you are going to write about.

Outline

Write a plan for what you are going to write. Include the main points you want to cover and the order you will cover them.

Writing and Editing Checklist

After you finish writing your essay, you can use this guide to review and edit your work. Use the questions as a guide to finding ways you can improve your work.

Writing Checklist

- ✓ Does your work have a strong opening? Does it introduce the topic and the main ideas?
- ✓ Is your work well-organized? Is related information grouped together? Does each paragraph have one main idea?
- ✓ Have you included facts, details, and examples to support your ideas?
- ✓ Is your work focused? Are there any details that do not fit with your main ideas?
- ✓ Do your ideas flow well? Have you used words and phrases to link ideas well?
- ✓ Does your work have a strong ending?

Editing Checklist

- ✓ Have you used a variety of sentence structures? Are your sentences all written correctly?
- ✓ Is the grammar correct?
- ✓ Are all words spelled correctly? You can check the spelling of any words you are not sure of.
- ✓ Is punctuation used correctly?
- ✓ Are all words capitalized correctly?

Reading and Writing

Practice Set 4

This practice set contains four writing tasks. These are described below.

Task 1: Short Passage with Questions

This task has a short passage followed by questions. Read each question carefully. Then write your answer in the space provided.

You can also practice writing skills by completing the Core Writing Skills Practice exercise.

Task 2: Short Passage with Questions

This task has a short passage followed by questions. Read each question carefully. Then write your answer in the space provided.

You can also practice writing skills by completing the Core Writing Skills Practice exercise.

Task 3: Argument Writing Task

This task requires you to write an argument. Read the writing prompt, complete the planning page, and then write or type your answer.

Task 4: Short Story Writing Task

This task requires you to write a short story. Read the writing prompt, complete the planning page, and then write or type your answer.

Task 1: Short Passage with Questions

Nana's Cookie Jar

I do love Nana's cookie jar.
The cookies are so enticing.
They're so chewy and so gooey.
Not like those hard pre-packed cookies
you can buy in any store.

Nana's choc chip cookies
have choc chips that are still warm and soft.
Then there are the ones
with the pink sticky icing!
Oh, don't forget the fruity ones,
and the fresh and fruity jam tarts!
They're like bursts of sunshine.
Yep, I do love Nana's cookie jar.

CORE WRITING SKILLS PRACTICE

The author gives details to help the reader imagine the cookies. Now imagine that you have tasted a cookie. Write a paragraph describing the taste. Use details and imagery to help the reader imagine the taste.

_____

_____

_____

_____

_____

1   Describe **two** ways Nana's cookies are different from pre-packed cookies.

1: _____

_____

2: _____

_____

2   Identify **one** example of internal rhyme, **one** example of alliteration, and **one** simile used in the poem.

Hint

Internal rhyme is when words within a line rhyme. Alliteration is when neighboring words start with the same consonant sound. A simile is when two objects are compared using the word *like* or *as*.

Internal rhyme: _____

_____

Alliteration: _____

_____

Simile: _____

_____

Task 2: Short Passage with Questions

Like a Rolling Stone

The Rolling Stones are one of the most successful rock and roll groups ever. After forming in London in April 1962, The Rolling Stones have stood the test of time. They have released over 30 successful albums, and have sold over 200 million albums worldwide.

They are even still playing today, led by original vocalist Mick Jagger and guitarist Keith Richards. Among The Rolling Stones' many popular songs are "You Can't Always Get What You Want" and "Paint It, Black." Many of their songs have also been covered by other bands and artists.

CORE WRITING SKILLS PRACTICE

Choose a band that you like and research it. Find out the answers to the questions below.

Band: _____

Who are the members of the band?

_____

Where and when did the band form?

_____

What sort of music do the band play?

_____

What are the band's biggest hit songs?

_____

---

1   How do you think the author feels about The Rolling Stones? Explain how you can tell.

Hint   Authors often have feelings about what they are writing about. You can guess how authors feel by what they write, by the words and phrases they use, and by their tone.

_____

_____

_____

_____

_____

_____

2   List **two** details the author includes to support the idea that The Rolling Stones were a successful rock and roll group.

1: _____

_____

2: _____

_____

Task 3: Argument Writing Task

Directions: Read the writing prompt below. Use the planning page to plan your writing. Then write or type your answer.

One of your teachers at school always gives a lot of homework. You feel that it is too much, and that it isn't giving you enough time to study all your subjects.

Write a letter to your teacher about the situation. Try to persuade your teacher to give the class less homework. Use reasons, facts, and/or examples to persuade your teacher.

Hint

A letter written to persuade needs to use good supporting details. You should state the main problem, but you should also explain why it is a problem.

In this letter, you should describe how all the homework affects you. You might describe how it stresses you, how you stay up too late and do not get enough sleep, or how you do not have enough time for other activities.

The key to a good persuasive letter is to use specific examples and details that will help the teacher understand why having too much homework is a problem.

Planning Page

Summary
Write a brief summary of your claim.

Supporting Details
Write down the facts, details, or examples you are going to include.

Outline
Write a plan for what you are going to write. Include the main points you want to cover and the order you will cover them.

Task 4: Short Story Writing Task

Directions: Read the writing prompt below. Use the planning page to plan your writing. Then write or type your answer.

Joel and Polly wanted to buy a drum kit. They came up with a plan to make the money.

Write a story about how Joel and Polly make the money to buy a drum kit.

Hint

A good story has a beginning, middle, and end. As you plan your story, focus on what is going to happen in each part.

The beginning often introduces the characters, the setting, and the main problem. The start of this story might describe Joel and Polly thinking of their plan.

The middle of the story might describe how they carry out the plan. This will be the main part of your story. It will usually be 2 or 3 paragraphs long. In this part, describe the events that take place.

At the end of the story, there should be some sort of conclusion. This could be Joel and Polly making enough money to buy their drum kit. It could have another ending such as Joel and Polly deciding that they do not want a drum kit after all. The conclusion should tie up the story and make it a complete story.

Planning Page

The Story
Write a summary of your story.

The Beginning
Describe what is going to happen at the start of your story.

The Middle
Describe what is going to happen in the middle of your story.

The End
Describe what is going to happen at the end of your story.

Writing and Editing Checklist

After you finish writing your story, you can use this guide to review and edit your work. Use the questions as a guide to finding ways you can improve your work.

Writing Checklist

- ✓ Does your story have a strong opening? Does it introduce the characters, the setting, or events well?
- ✓ Is your story well-organized? Do the events flow well?
- ✓ Does your story have an effective ending? Does it tie up the story well?
- ✓ Does your story include dialogue? If not, could dialogue make your story better?
- ✓ Have you used strong words? Are there words that could be replaced with better ones?
- ✓ Have you used effective descriptions? Could your descriptions be improved?
- ✓ Have you used sensory details? Could you add more sensory details to help readers imagine the scene?

Editing Checklist

- ✓ Have you used a variety of sentence structures? Are your sentences all written correctly?
- ✓ Is the grammar correct?
- ✓ Are all words spelled correctly? You can check the spelling of any words you are not sure of.
- ✓ Is punctuation used correctly?
- ✓ If dialogue is used, is it punctuated correctly?
- ✓ Are all words capitalized correctly?

Reading and Writing

Practice Set 5

This practice set contains four writing tasks. These are described below.

Task 1: Short Passage with Questions

This task has a short passage followed by questions. Read each question carefully. Then write your answer in the space provided.

You can also practice writing skills by completing the Core Writing Skills Practice exercise.

Task 2: Short Passage with Questions

This task has a short passage followed by questions. Read each question carefully. Then write your answer in the space provided.

You can also practice writing skills by completing the Core Writing Skills Practice exercise.

Task 3: Long Passage with Essay Question

This task has a longer passage with an essay question. Read the passage, complete the planning page, and then write or type your answer.

Task 4: Explanatory Writing Task

This final task requires you to write an essay that explains something. Read the writing prompt, complete the planning page, and then write or type your answer.

Task 1: Short Passage with Questions

Amelia Earhart

Born in 1897, Amelia Earhart is an American aviation pioneer. She was the first woman to fly solo across the Atlantic Ocean. At that time, it was rare for females to be pilots, let alone be record-breaking pilots! Earhart set many other aviation records during her life, and also wrote about her experiences. She became a celebrity in the United States, and appeared in many advertisements.

The Purdue University funded an ill-fated flight of the globe in 1937. Sadly, Amelia Earhart and her navigator disappeared over the central Pacific Ocean. To this day, it is unknown what actually happened. Some researchers believe that the plane crashed into the ocean and sank. Another theory is that Amelia landed at an uninhabited island called Gardner Island. There have been many other theories, but none have yet to be proven. It may never be known what happened to Amelia Earhart. However, she can still always be remembered as a great pilot who achieved many incredible things.

CORE WRITING SKILLS PRACTICE
WRITE A RESEARCH REPORT

Amelia Earhart is one woman who achieved great things in aviation. Research the three women below. Write each woman's main achievement below. Then write a report that describes how women have achieved great things in aviation. Use details about the three women below and about Amelia Earhart in your report.

Harriet Quimby _____

Amy Johnson _____

Geraldine Mock _____

1   Why was Amelia Earhart a pioneer? Use details from the passage in your answer.

Hint   Think about what the word *pioneer* means. Then describe in what way Amelia Earhart was a pioneer.

_____

_____

_____

_____

_____

2   What is the main purpose of the second paragraph? Use details from the passage to support your answer.

_____

_____

_____

_____

_____

Task 2: Short Passage with Questions

Disappearing Dessert

It was a windy autumn morning in the backstreets of Brooklyn, New York. Tony was walking to the barber shop carrying a brown paper bag filled with cannoli. Along the way, he stopped to talk with Vinnie at the newspaper stand and gave him a few cannolis. Tony said goodbye and continued on toward the barber shop.

He had nearly arrived when he ran into Jen. The two spoke for a while and Tony gave Jen a handful of cannolis to eat for dessert that evening. Just around the corner from the barber shop, he saw Mr. Jackson walking his dog. He raced over to say hello, and then offered Mr. Jackson a cannoli. Tony finally made it to the barber shop.

"Uncle Benny! Here are the delicious cannolis you asked Mamma to make for you!" Tony exclaimed.

He handed over the brown paper bag to his Uncle Benny and left the shop to go back home. Uncle Benny looked into the bag to find nothing inside.

"There are no cannolis in here," he grumbled.

© John Mueller

CORE WRITING SKILLS PRACTICE
WRITE A SHORT STORY

In this story, Tony creates a problem because he is too nice. Think of another situation where being too nice might create a problem. Briefly describe the situation below. Then write a short story about the situation.

How is the person too nice? _____

What happens because the person is too nice? _____

_____

1   Write a summary of the events of the passage.

> **Hint**   A summary should describe the main events of a passage. It should include only the important events or details.

_____

_____

_____

_____

_____

2   Explain how the author creates humor in the passage. Use details from the passage to support your answer.

_____

_____

_____

_____

_____

3   Why is the bag that Tony gives Uncle Benny empty? Use details from the passage in your answer.

Hint   To answer this question, you have to describe what happens in the passage. Explain what Tony does and why this causes the bag to be empty when he gives it to Uncle Benny.

_____

_____

_____

_____

_____

_____

_____

_____

_____

_____

_____

_____

Writing and Editing Checklist

After you finish writing your answer to question 3, you can use this guide to review and edit your work. Use the questions as a guide to finding ways you can improve your work.

Writing Checklist

- ✓ Does your work have a strong opening? Does it introduce the topic and the main ideas?
- ✓ Is your work well-organized? Is related information grouped together? Does each paragraph have one main idea?
- ✓ Have you clearly explained what Tony does and how it causes the bag to be empty? Have you used details from the passage to support your answer?
- ✓ Is your work focused? Are there any details that do not fit with your main ideas?
- ✓ Do your ideas flow well? Have you used words and phrases to link ideas well?

Editing Checklist

- ✓ Have you used a variety of sentence structures? Are your sentences all written correctly?
- ✓ Is the grammar correct?
- ✓ Are all words spelled correctly? You can check the spelling of any words you are not sure of.
- ✓ Is punctuation used correctly?
- ✓ If dialogue is used, is it punctuated correctly?
- ✓ Are all words capitalized correctly?

Task 3: Long Passage with Essay Question

Directions: Read the passage below. Then answer the question that follows. Use the planning page to plan your writing. Then write or type your essay.

The Sporting Chance Academy

Are you tired of video games and lazy summer afternoons? Are you keen to have a more active lifestyle? The Sporting Chance Academy gives you the chance to play your favorite sport and make new friends. It is open between March and October and can be joined by anyone between the ages of 10 and 18. The academy is suitable whether you dream of a career as a professional sportsperson, or simply want to enjoy a recreational game with other young people. Whatever your goals for joining are, the Sporting Chance Academy can help you to achieve them.

Learn to Play Regardless of Your Goals

If you wish to play sport as a future career, then the academy holds many possibilities. Our team has former basketball, baseball, and NFL professionals on hand to teach you the arts of each game. These individuals also have influence in the professional game and will help to progress your talents. Such an environment can help you to build a network of contacts in your sport of choice. Joining the Sporting Chance Academy may even be the springboard to a long and successful professional career.

The academy has also done great work in the local community. It offers an outlet to high school students who are either uninspired or not engaged by their classes. By allowing them to participate in disciplined sport and training, it lets them focus their energy positively. Many students have attended the academy and developed a love for sport. Others have even gone on to achieve scholarships in baseball and college football. Our academy prides itself on giving students an opportunity to shine and make the most of their abilities.

Creating a Generation of Fit and Healthy Adults

Of course, some of our visitors simply attend the academy for fun. If you are looking to participate in sport for pleasure, then our facilities are especially suitable. Even with an element of competition the academy's aim is to make sport both fun and appealing to youths. This means that you can still enjoy our activities and stay fit even if your true passion lies elsewhere. We pride ourselves on being accessible to anyone who wants to enjoy a new experience. So don't be deterred if you do not consider yourself to be the sporting type! You'll still find that the academy is a welcoming place where you can take on activities that suit your needs and skills.

It is our mission to bring sport to the next generation of adults. We believe that outdoor recreation can replace video games as the preferred choice of entertainment in the future. This can lead to a fitter and healthier generation who can live active and energetic lives. The Sporting Chance Academy believes in better children of today and the adults of tomorrow. If you wish to participate, then please visit our website or telephone us today. Our representatives are waiting to hear from you.

1   Do you think the Sporting Chance Academy would be a good academy for you to attend? Explain why or why not.

In your answer, be sure to

- give your opinion on whether the Sporting Chance Academy would be a good academy for you to attend
- explain why you would or would not want to attend the academy
- use details from the passage
- write an answer of between 1 and 2 pages

Hint

This question is asking you to write a personal response to the passage. You have to decide whether you would or would not like to attend the academy. Once you have made your decision, think of 2 or 3 reasons to support it. If you would like to attend, describe 2 or 3 benefits you think you would gain by attending the academy. You can use the benefits described in the passage in this part of your answer. If you would not like to attend, give 2 or 3 reasons why.

Planning Page

Summary
Write a brief summary of what you are going to write about.

Supporting Details
Write down the facts, details, or examples you are going to include in your answer.

Outline
Write a plan for what you are going to write. Include the main points you want to cover and the order you will cover them.

Task 4: Explanatory Writing Task

Directions: Read the writing prompt below. Use the planning page to plan your writing. Then write or type your answer.

The Wiggly Worm

The worm is one of nature's
most wonderful of creatures,
as it slinks beneath the soil,
with all its special features.

Though they barely see above the grass,
they see all beneath the ground,
hiding amongst the flower beds,
as they wiggle round and round.

In "The Wiggly Worm," the poet describes an animal that she finds interesting and amazing. What animal do you think is special? What makes that animal special? Write an essay that explains why the animal you have chosen is special.

Hint

This writing task introduces the topic by using a poem. You do not have to refer to the poem in your answer. The poem is just there to help you start thinking about the topic.

The goal of your writing is to write about an animal that you think is special. In your essay, you should give details about the animal and explain why it is special.

Planning Page

Summary

Write a brief summary of what you are going to write about.

Outline

Write a plan for what you are going to write. Include the main points you want to cover and the order you will cover them.

Writing and Editing Checklist

After you finish writing your essay, you can use this guide to review and edit your work. Use the questions as a guide to finding ways you can improve your work.

Writing Checklist

- ✓ Does your work have a strong opening? Does it introduce the topic and the main ideas?
- ✓ Is your work well-organized? Is related information grouped together? Does each paragraph have one main idea?
- ✓ Have you included facts, details, and examples to support your ideas?
- ✓ Is your work focused? Are there any details that do not fit with your main ideas?
- ✓ Do your ideas flow well? Have you used words and phrases to link ideas well?
- ✓ Does your work have a strong ending?

Editing Checklist

- ✓ Have you used a variety of sentence structures? Are your sentences all written correctly?
- ✓ Is the grammar correct?
- ✓ Are all words spelled correctly? You can check the spelling of any words you are not sure of.
- ✓ Is punctuation used correctly?
- ✓ Are all words capitalized correctly?

Reading and Writing

Practice Set 6

This practice set contains four writing tasks. These are described below.

Task 1: Short Passage with Questions

This task has a short passage followed by questions. Read each question carefully. Then write your answer in the space provided.

You can also practice writing skills by completing the Core Writing Skills Practice exercise.

Task 2: Short Passage with Questions

This task has a short passage followed by questions. Read each question carefully. Then write your answer in the space provided.

You can also practice writing skills by completing the Core Writing Skills Practice exercise.

Task 3: Short Story Writing Task

This task requires you to write a short story. Read the writing prompt, complete the planning page, and then write or type your answer.

Task 4: Argument Writing Task

This final task requires you to write an argument. Read the writing prompt, complete the planning page, and then write or type your answer.

Task 1: Short Passage with Questions

Nintendo

Did you know that Nintendo didn't always make video game consoles? Before the first Nintendo gaming console was ever thought of, Nintendo was making playing cards!

Nintendo was originally founded in 1889 to make playing cards for a game called Hanafuda. Nintendo later tried many different business ideas before finding its niche. These included a taxi company, a television network, and a food company.

All of Nintendo's earlier business ventures failed. It was not until 1983 when Nintendo launched the original Nintendo Entertainment System (NES) that the company found commercial success. A handheld game console called the Game Boy followed in 1989.

The Nintendo DS and the Nintendo Wii were both highly successful.

It has since gone on to make other similar products. The Nintendo DS was released in 2004 and has sold over 150 million units. The Nintendo Wii was launched in 2006. It was a gaming system that was able to sense the movements of players, and use the movements to direct the game. For example, someone playing tennis would swing the controller to cause the player in the game to swing the tennis racket. The Wii sold over 90 million units in less than 5 years.

CORE WRITING SKILLS PRACTICE

What lesson does the passage have about not giving up? Explain your answer.

_____

_____

_____

_____

1   Complete the web below using information from the passage.

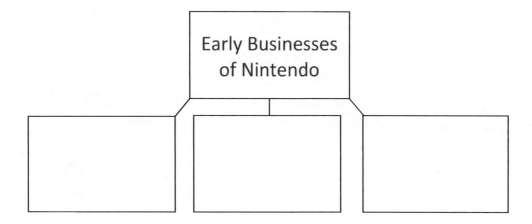

2   List the entertainment products created by Nintendo in the order they were created.

This question is asking you to summarize the information given on the entertainment products released in sequence. Write a summary by listing the name of the product, the year it was released, and what it did.

_____

_____

_____

_____

_____

_____

Task 2: Short Passage with Questions

The Fox and the Hound

First published in 1967, *The Fox and the Hound* is a novel written by American novelist Daniel P. Mannix. The story follows the life of a red fox named Tod and his run-ins with Copper, a dog owned by a local hunter. During the year of its release, the novel was the winner of a number of literary awards.

Walt Disney Pictures eventually purchased the film rights to *The Fox and the Hound* and a film adaptation began production in 1977. At the time, it was the most expensive animated film ever made. It was released in 1981 and was very successful.

The film *The Fox and the Hound 2* was released in 2006. It was not as successful as the original. However, the story was still enchanting and entertaining.

The film's original poster.

CORE WRITING SKILLS PRACTICE

The passage describes events in order. Summarize the passage by completing the timeline below.

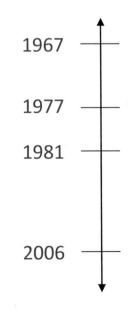

1967

1977

1981

2006

---

1   Describe **two** facts and **two** opinions given in the passage.

Fact 1: _____

_____

Fact 2: _____

_____

Opinion 1: _____

_____

Opinion 2: _____

_____

2   The author states that *The Fox and the Hound 2* was not as successful as the original film. Describe some facts or details the author could include to support this statement.

_____

_____

_____

_____

_____

Task 3: Short Story Writing Task

Directions: Read the writing prompt below. Use the planning page to plan your writing. Then write or type your answer.

Look at the picture below.

Write a story based on what is happening in the picture.

Your story should be based on the picture given. You should use the picture to come up with an idea for your story. The story shows a group of people whitewater rafting. Start with this and think of something that could happen while the people are rafting. Make sure you come up with a complete story.

Planning Page

The Story
Write a summary of your story.

The Beginning
Describe what is going to happen at the start of your story.

The Middle
Describe what is going to happen in the middle of your story.

The End
Describe what is going to happen at the end of your story.

Task 4: Argument Writing Task

Directions: Read the writing prompt below. Use the planning page to plan your writing. Then write or type your answer.

Read this proverb about first impressions.

First impressions are the most lasting.

Do you agree with this proverb? Explain why or why not. Use facts, details, or examples in your answer.

Hint

A proverb is a short saying that states an idea. This proverb describes how people do not forget their first impression of someone. You have to explain whether or not you agree with this.

When you are asked whether or not you agree with something, you will not be scored based on whether you agree or not. You will be scored on how well you explain why you do or do not agree. Don't worry about choosing the right answer. Instead, focus on what your personal opinion is. Then focus on clearly explaining why this is your opinion.

Planning Page

Summary
Write a brief summary of your claim.

Supporting Details
Write down the facts, details, or examples you are going to include.

Outline
Write a plan for what you are going to write. Include the main points you want to cover and the order you will cover them.

Writing and Editing Checklist

After you finish writing your argument, you can use this guide to review and edit your work. Use the questions as a guide to finding ways you can improve your work.

Writing Checklist

- ✓ Does your work have one clear claim?
- ✓ Does your work have a strong opening? Does the opening introduce the topic and state the claim?
- ✓ Is your claim supported? Have you used clear reasons to support your claim?
- ✓ Have you used enough evidence? Is your evidence all relevant?
- ✓ Is your work well-organized? Is related information grouped together? Does each paragraph have one main idea?
- ✓ Do your ideas flow well? Have you used words and phrases to link ideas well?
- ✓ Does your work have a strong ending? Does the ending restate the main idea and tie up the argument?

Editing Checklist

- ✓ Have you used a variety of sentence structures? Are your sentences all written correctly?
- ✓ Is the grammar correct?
- ✓ Are all words spelled correctly? You can check the spelling of any words you are not sure of.
- ✓ Is punctuation used correctly?
- ✓ Are all words capitalized correctly?

Reading and Writing

Practice Set 7

This practice set contains four writing tasks. These are described below.

Task 1: Short Passage with Questions

This task has a short passage followed by questions. Read each question carefully. Then write your answer in the space provided.

You can also practice writing skills by completing the Core Writing Skills Practice exercise.

Task 2: Short Passage with Questions

This task has a short passage followed by questions. Read each question carefully. Then write your answer in the space provided.

You can also practice writing skills by completing the Core Writing Skills Practice exercise.

Task 3: Long Passage with Essay Question

This task has a longer passage with an essay question. Read the passage, complete the planning page, and then write or type your answer.

Task 4: Explanatory Writing Task

This final task requires you to write an essay that explains something. Read the writing prompt, complete the planning page, and then write or type your answer.

Task 1: Short Passage with Questions

Tau Ceti

Tau Ceti is a large star located within the Cetus constellation. It is similar to our Sun in both mass and spectral type. It is located at just under 12 light years from our Solar System, and can be seen by the naked eye. Because it is so much like our Sun, many scientists believed that it could have a planet similar to Earth orbiting it. If that planet had the right conditions, it could be home to a form of life. Tau Ceti has been the focus of extensive searches for extraterrestrial life.

In 2004, Jane Greaves and her team of astronomers discovered that Tau Ceti has almost 10 times more debris orbiting it than our own Sun. This means that the planet would be impacted by meteors quite often. Due to this debris, the possibility of finding evidence of life surrounding the star is very unlikely. However, Tau Ceti is still often used in science fiction books and films as a solar system found to have life.

CORE WRITING SKILLS PRACTICE

The passage uses several scientific terms. Look up the meaning of the three terms below. Write your own definition of the terms.

constellation: _____

_____

spectral type: _____

_____

light year: _____

_____

---

1   Compare and contrast the Sun and Tau Ceti.

Hint   Be sure to describe ways the Sun and Tau Ceti are similar and ways the Sun and Tau Ceti are different.

_____

_____

_____

_____

_____

2   How did Jane Greaves' findings most likely affect beliefs about Tau Ceti possibly being home to a form of life?

_____

_____

_____

_____

_____

Task 2: Short Passage with Questions

The Highest Price

The bell chimed at the entry door to the Captain's quarters.

"Come," Captain Ludikar beckoned.

The door slid open and in walked Commander Sever.

"Captain, just checking if you're okay," Sever said with concern in his voice.

Ludikar smirked and turned toward Sever.

"We may have lost a lot of good people today. Am I okay? Yes. I'm okay because I'm still here. The problem is I don't know if they're okay. They're down there on that planet, our mission failed today, and now we can't pick them up until morning. That is what's bothering me," Captain Ludikar replied.

"They're well-trained, well-prepared, and I feel sure they will survive the night. Meanwhile, we're preparing to go in and pick them up at first light tomorrow. Rest easy, Captain. We have this under control," Commander Sever replied.

Captain Ludikar nodded and tried to smile, but he knew he would be getting little sleep until he knew that his people were safe.

CORE WRITING SKILLS PRACTICE
WRITE A SHORT STORY

Imagine you are one of the people left on the planet until morning. Write a brief description of what happens during the night. Then write a short story that describes your night on the planet.

_____

_____

_____

1   Support the statement below using details from the passage.

Captain Ludikar is a loyal captain who cares about his people.

_____

_____

_____

_____

_____

2   What genre is the passage? Explain how you can tell.

Hint   Genre refers to the category a work of literature falls into. Common genres include mystery, fantasy, horror, adventure, science fiction, and historical fiction.

_____

_____

_____

_____

Task 3: Long Passage with Essay Question

Directions: Read the passage below. Then answer the question that follows. Use the planning page to plan your writing. Then write or type your essay.

The Choice

Stephen and Marcus were typical brothers. They would argue about anything and everything, and they were very competitive when they played together. Any discussion about their favorite basketball team or television program would end in a disagreement. This was made worse because they shared a room together. This meant that even when they went to bed, they would argue long into the night. Their father would often have to come into their room at night to make sure they got to sleep.

One day their mother brought them a new DVD player. They each got a new DVD to watch as well. The boys were excited and couldn't wait to sit down and watch their programs. Of course their excitement meant that they couldn't agree on who should watch their DVD first.

"I should go first because I'm older," said Stephen.

"But I should watch mine first because I am younger and have to go to bed earlier," Marcus retorted.

They argued for almost an hour before their mother decided to step in.

"This is silly boys," she said. "I know how to settle this."

She took the DVD player and placed it on the table. Then she took the two DVDs and put them at the other end of the table.

"Since you cannot seem to share the DVD player, it now belongs just to Stephen," she explained.

Stephen clapped his hands. Marcus was just about the protest, but his mother stopped him.

"Don't worry Marcus," she said. "You are now the proud sole owner of both the DVDs."

The boys both grinned at first. Then their grins gradually faded as they realized that there was something wrong with this agreement. The boys looked at each other in confusion.

"But I can't watch anything if I don't own a single DVD," Stephen said.

"And I have two DVDS, but I can't watch either one without a DVD player," Marcus added. "We can't choose between them because we need both or we can't use either."

"I know," said their mother. "Maybe the best way to solve this problem is to learn to share."

Stephen sighed. Marcus let a gentle smile light up his face.

"Okay," said Stephen. "I suppose that Marcus can watch his program first."

Marcus's smile became even wider and he thanked his brother. Their mother smiled as Marcus began to play his DVD. She wasn't convinced that the boys had really learned their lesson, but at least they were peaceful for the moment.

1   At the start of the passage, the brothers are both being selfish. Think of a time when someone you know was being selfish. Describe who was selfish, what they did that was selfish, and how you felt about it.

In your answer, be sure to
- describe a time when someone you know was being selfish
- describe who was selfish and what they did that was selfish
- explain how you felt about the situation
- write an answer of between 1 and 2 pages

This question asks you to relate to the passage. You have to write about your own experience of knowing somebody who acted in a selfish way.

To answer this question, it is important to first think of one specific example. Don't try to write about more than one person or more than one event. You may think of someone who is often selfish. To keep your answer focused, think of one specific example of a time that the person was selfish. Focus on clearly describing how the person was selfish and how it affected you.

Planning Page

Summary
Write a brief summary of what you are going to write about.

Supporting Details
Write down the facts, details, or examples you are going to include in your answer.

Outline
Write a plan for what you are going to write. Include the main points you want to cover and the order you will cover them.

Task 4: Explanatory Writing Task

Directions: Read the writing prompt below. Use the planning page to plan your writing. Then write or type your answer.

Think about the town or city where you live. What makes the town or city where you live special? What do you like about the place where you live?

Write a composition describing the town or city where you live. Explain what makes the town or city special.

Hint

When planning your writing, it is a good idea to break down what you want to say into paragraphs. This will help make sure your writing is well-organized and easy to understand. In your outline, describe what you are going to cover in each paragraph. Make sure that each paragraph has one main idea.

In this essay, each paragraph might focus on one thing that makes your town special. Another idea is to state a main idea in the first paragraph, such as by saying that all the people in your town know and help each other. Each paragraph could then give one example of how the people in the town help each other.

Planning Page

Summary

Write a brief summary of what you are going to write about.

Outline

Write a plan for what you are going to write. Include the main points you want to cover and the order you will cover them.

Writing and Editing Checklist

After you finish writing your essay, you can use this guide to review and edit your work. Use the questions as a guide to finding ways you can improve your work.

Writing Checklist

- ✓ Does your work have a strong opening? Does it introduce the topic and the main ideas?
- ✓ Is your work well-organized? Is related information grouped together? Does each paragraph have one main idea?
- ✓ Have you included facts, details, and examples to support your ideas?
- ✓ Is your work focused? Are there any details that do not fit with your main ideas?
- ✓ Do your ideas flow well? Have you used words and phrases to link ideas well?
- ✓ Does your work have a strong ending?

Editing Checklist

- ✓ Have you used a variety of sentence structures? Are your sentences all written correctly?
- ✓ Is the grammar correct?
- ✓ Are all words spelled correctly? You can check the spelling of any words you are not sure of.
- ✓ Is punctuation used correctly?
- ✓ Are all words capitalized correctly?

Reading and Writing

Practice Set 8

This practice set contains four writing tasks. These are described below.

Task 1: Short Passage with Questions

This task has a short passage followed by questions. Read each question carefully. Then write your answer in the space provided.

You can also practice writing skills by completing the Core Writing Skills Practice exercise.

Task 2: Short Passage with Questions

This task has a short passage followed by questions. Read each question carefully. Then write your answer in the space provided.

You can also practice writing skills by completing the Core Writing Skills Practice exercise.

Task 3: Argument Writing Task

This task requires you to write an argument. Read the writing prompt, complete the planning page, and then write or type your answer.

Task 4: Short Story Writing Task

This task requires you to write a short story. Read the writing prompt, complete the planning page, and then write or type your answer.

Task 1: Short Passage with Questions

Michelangelo

Born in 1475, Michelangelo was a genius of both academics and artistry. He lived during the Renaissance, which was a time in Europe when art was thriving. He was considered a typical Renaissance man. This term refers to people who have talents in many different areas. While he is best known as an artist and sculptor, he was also a poet, an engineer, and an architect.

Michelangelo's work became renowned pieces of his time period. The statue of David, completed in 1504, is arguably one of Michelangelo's most famous works. It was sculpted from marble, and took over two years to complete.

A less known fact about the statue is that it was originally intended to be placed on the roof of the Florence Cathedral. Just before it was complete, people realized that placing it on the Florence Cathedral would be impossible. The statue weighed over 6 ton. While the roof would probably be able to support the weight, it would have been almost impossible to lift the statue. This was in the 1500s before cranes and other machines would have made the task a lot simpler!

The statue was placed in a public square in Florence instead. It can be found today at the Academy of Fine Arts in Florence, but visitors to Florence can also see a replica of the famous statue where it was originally placed.

CORE WRITING SKILLS PRACTICE

Do you think the author admires Michelangelo? Explain how you can tell.

_____

_____

_____

1   Why was Michelangelo a "typical Renaissance man"?

Hint   The passage defines what a typical Renaissance man was. Use this definition in your answer, and explain why Michelangelo matches the definition.

_____

_____

_____

_____

_____

_____

2   Why wasn't the statue placed on the roof of the Florence Cathedral? Use details from the passage to support your answer.

_____

_____

_____

_____

_____

Task 2: Short Passage with Questions

The students in Jack's class were asked to write a short essay about an inspiring person from their town. Jack wrote this essay about Dr. Price.

A Helping Hand

Dr. Price is always trying to help different people in different parts of the world. Recently, he flew to Japan to help the local doctors and aid teams after a large earthquake shook their country. The year before, he traveled to Africa to provide healthcare to people living in poverty.

Dr. Price is a wealthy and successful doctor in our town, and his services are always in demand. But he never forgets how important it is to help people less fortunate. Dr. Price has always believed that many people taking small steps can make a big difference. We may not all be able to do what Dr. Price does, but we can all learn from his example and find a way to help others.

CORE WRITING SKILLS PRACTICE
WRITE A PERSUASIVE ESSAY

Choose someone you know who inspires you. Answer the questions below about that person. Then write an essay explaining to others why the person you have chosen is inspiring.

Who do you find inspiring?

_____

What does the person do that makes them inspiring?

_____

What can others learn from the person?

_____

1   Do you agree that Dr. Price is an inspirational person? Explain why or why not.

Hint   This question is asking for your personal opinion. You may agree or you may disagree. However, be sure to describe why you have that opinion.

_____

_____

_____

_____

_____

2   Circle the word below that best describes Dr. Price. Then explain why you chose that word.

selfless   **generous**

_____

_____

_____

_____

_____

_____

3   Jack writes in his essay that "we can all learn from his example." What do you think people can learn from Dr. Price? Use details from the passage in your answer.

Hint

Think about how Dr. Price's actions can apply to all people. In your answer, describe one or two key things that people can learn from Dr. Price. In questions like this, you can also write about what you personally learned from Dr. Price.

_____

_____

_____

_____

_____

_____

_____

_____

_____

_____

_____

Writing and Editing Checklist

After you finish writing your answer to question 3, you can use this guide to review and edit your work. Use the questions as a guide to finding ways you can improve your work.

Writing Checklist

- ✓ Does your work have a strong opening? Does it introduce the topic and the main ideas?
- ✓ Is your work well-organized? Is related information grouped together? Does each paragraph have one main idea?
- ✓ Have you clearly explained what people can learn from Dr. Price? Have you used details from the passage to support your claims?
- ✓ Is your work focused? Are there any details that do not fit with your main ideas?
- ✓ Do your ideas flow well? Have you used words and phrases to link ideas well?

Editing Checklist

- ✓ Have you used a variety of sentence structures? Are your sentences all written correctly?
- ✓ Is the grammar correct?
- ✓ Are all words spelled correctly? You can check the spelling of any words you are not sure of.
- ✓ Is punctuation used correctly?
- ✓ If dialogue is used, is it punctuated correctly?
- ✓ Are all words capitalized correctly?

Task 3: Argument Writing Task

Directions: Read the writing prompt below. Use the planning page to plan your writing. Then write or type your answer.

The town you live in has plans to build a series of bicycle tracks. The tracks will cost a lot of money, but they will allow people to safely ride all around town. You decide to write a letter to your local newspaper expressing your opinion on the plan.

Write a letter to your newspaper expressing your opinion on whether or not the bicycle track should be built. Use reasons, facts, and/or examples to support your opinion.

Hint

When completing these writing tasks, it is important to include supporting details. In some tasks, you can use facts. In a task like this, it is often better to use details and examples.

Once you have decided whether or not you think the bicycle track is a good idea, think of details and examples you can use to support your opinion. Keep your letter organized by having each paragraph focused on one supporting detail.

Planning Page

Summary
Write a brief summary of your claim.

Supporting Details
Write down the facts, details, or examples you are going to include.

Outline
Write a plan for what you are going to write. Include the main points you want to cover and the order you will cover them.

Task 4: Short Story Writing Task

Directions: Read the writing prompt below. Use the planning page to plan your writing. Then write or type your answer.

Look at the picture below.

Write a story based on what is happening in the picture.

Many stories are based on a problem that occurs. The problem becomes the basis of the story's plot.

Think of a problem these characters are having. For example, they could be running last in a race or they could be lost. They could be about to be chased by a wolf or one of the characters could be about to slip over and sprain an ankle.

Think of a problem and base your story around it. The first part of the story will introduce the problem. The middle part will tell how the characters solve the problem. The ending will tie up the story by solving the problem.

Planning Page

The Story
Write a summary of your story.

The Beginning
Describe what is going to happen at the start of your story.

The Middle
Describe what is going to happen in the middle of your story.

The End
Describe what is going to happen at the end of your story.

Writing and Editing Checklist

After you finish writing your story, you can use this guide to review and edit your work. Use the questions as a guide to finding ways you can improve your work.

Writing Checklist

- ✓ Does your story have a strong opening? Does it introduce the characters, the setting, or events well?
- ✓ Is your story well-organized? Do the events flow well?
- ✓ Does your story have an effective ending? Does it tie up the story well?
- ✓ Does your story include dialogue? If not, could dialogue make your story better?
- ✓ Have you used strong words? Are there words that could be replaced with better ones?
- ✓ Have you used effective descriptions? Could your descriptions be improved?
- ✓ Have you used sensory details? Could you add more sensory details to help readers imagine the scene?

Editing Checklist

- ✓ Have you used a variety of sentence structures? Are your sentences all written correctly?
- ✓ Is the grammar correct?
- ✓ Are all words spelled correctly? You can check the spelling of any words you are not sure of.
- ✓ Is punctuation used correctly?
- ✓ If dialogue is used, is it punctuated correctly?
- ✓ Are all words capitalized correctly?

Reading and Writing

Practice Set 9

This practice set contains four writing tasks. These are described below.

Task 1: Short Passage with Questions

This task has a short passage followed by questions. Read each question carefully. Then write your answer in the space provided.

You can also practice writing skills by completing the Core Writing Skills Practice exercise.

Task 2: Short Passage with Questions

This task has a short passage followed by questions. Read each question carefully. Then write your answer in the space provided.

You can also practice writing skills by completing the Core Writing Skills Practice exercise.

Task 3: Long Passage with Essay Question

This task has a longer passage with an essay question. Read the passage, complete the planning page, and then write or type your answer.

Task 4: Personal Narrative Writing Task

This final task requires you to write a personal narrative. Read the writing prompt, complete the planning page, and then write or type your answer.

Task 1: Short Passage with Questions

Constantinople

The Fall of Constantinople occurred thousands of years ago. The historical event was an important turning point in history. It involved the capture of the capital of the Byzantine Empire by the Ottomans. This event took place in 1453. Before this, the Byzantine Empire had seemed unstoppable. It had been the most powerful and wealthiest empire in Europe for over five hundred years.

The Fall of Constantinople marked the end of Emperor Constantine XI's rule. It was also the end of the Byzantine Empire. After the conquest, Constantinople became the Ottoman Empire's new capital.

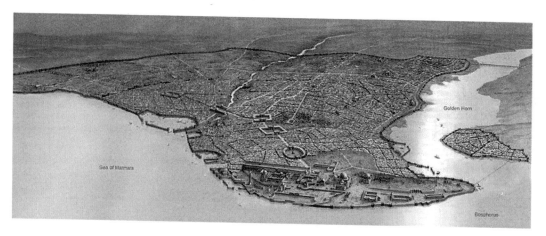

CORE SKILLS PRACTICE

How does the author support the idea that the Fall of Constantinople was an important turning point in history? Explain your answer.

_____

_____

_____

_____

1   What was the Fall of Constantinople?

Hint   This question is asking you to write a summary of the passage. Be sure not to write what the passage says word for word. Instead, use your own words to write your summary.

_____

_____

_____

_____

_____

_____

2   Describe **two** things that changed after the Fall of Constantinople. Use details from the passage in your answer.

1: _____

_____

2: _____

_____

Task 2: Short Passage with Questions

Poor King Henri

As the snow began to fall over the Halls of Alloric, King Henri became grumpy and quite bothersome to his loyal subjects. King Henri never meant to be so abrupt or abrasive. He did enjoy the company of his friends and fellows. It was just that all this cold made Henri's knee ache and throb constantly. It was the aching that he could not bear. He thought about the aching all day, and often snapped at the people around him. He tossed and turned all night, becoming more and more tired by the day. As the days became colder, King Henri's friends began to avoid him. He was often left alone, where he thought about his aching joints even more. By the end of winter, he was eating alone every night.

Then the spring would come and everything would change. King Henri would emerge from his grumpy loneliness like a flower blooming in the warmth of the spring sunshine. King Henri marked the occasion by throwing a large celebration. For days, a fabulous feast and festival would go on. All this was to thank everyone for being so understanding of his peculiar ways.

CORE WRITING SKILLS PRACTICE

The author says that King Henri "would emerge from his grumpy loneliness like a flower blooming in the warmth of the spring sunshine." Do you think this simile explains King Henri's change of mood well? Explain your answer.

_____

_____

_____

_____

_____

---

1   Why did King Henri feel worse as winter continued?

Hint   This is a cause and effect question. Describe how King Henri's initial grumpiness made things worse over time.

_____

_____

_____

_____

_____

2   Do you think the celebration made up for how King Henri treated everyone? Explain your answer.

_____

_____

_____

_____

_____

Task 3: Long Passage with Essay Question

Directions: Read the passage below. Then answer the question that follows. Use the planning page to plan your writing. Then write or type your essay.

Getting in Your Own Way

Samantha prided herself on being the cleverest girl in her class. She would always pass her exams and achieve good grades in every subject. Her friends often asked her for help, and she loved that her friends relied on her so much. Then one day, a new girl called Tabatha started at Samantha's school. She was the same age as Samantha and took part in all of her classes. Tabatha was also very clever and excelled in all of her studies. Tabatha was a very friendly girl who was making good friends with all of her classmates. Samantha liked her, but she was jealous that she was no longer the cleverest girl in the class. They often got similar results on tests, but Samantha still felt like Tabatha was smarter than her. After all, Tabatha spent a lot of her spare time having fun with her friends. She certainly didn't seemed stressed or overworked.

Soon it was time for the end of year exams. Samantha decided that she wanted to complete the exam and gain a better grade than Tabatha. She wanted to prove that she was smarter than Tabatha. "Don't worry about that," warned her mother. "You should just concentrate on your own work." But no matter how hard Samantha tried, she could not stop thinking about beating Tabatha.

When it came time for the exam, Samantha felt very tense. Tabatha was very relaxed and was joking with her friends before the test. Samantha was so tense she hardly said a word to anyone. As they filed into the exam, Samantha took a seat across the aisle from Tabatha. She didn't want Tabatha to see how nervous she was, so she leaned casually back in her chair and tried to act like she didn't even care. When the teacher announced that it was time to start work, Tabatha started right away. Samantha casually picked up her pencil and slowly opened her test book, while hoping that Tabatha would notice that she was in no rush at all.

As they settled down, Samantha felt distracted by Tabatha and struggled to pay attention to her questions. She started to focus eventually, but began to rush her answers. Samantha was determined to finish the exam well before Tabatha. Each question was answered in an even more hurried manner. Eventually she finished and left the exam hall with thirty minutes left to go. Tabatha looked up in surprise as Samantha walked past.

Then Tabatha put her head down, and did not look up again during the remainder of the exam. She finally completed her exam with just a minute left on the clock. As she left the hall, a soft smile lit up her face. She saw Samantha sitting by the main entrance.

"How do you think you did on the exam?" Tabatha asked.

Samantha paused before responding, and then mustered her most confident voice. "I think I did well, thanks! I finished with lots of time to spare."

"I just hope it went well," said Tabatha. "I took a lot longer than you so I may have struggled."

When the results were announced, Samantha had earned a B grade. She looked down at the score sadly. It wasn't too bad, but she knew that she could have done better. She peeked over at Tabatha's exam and saw that she had received an A. Samantha suddenly felt very angry at herself. She had wasted energy worrying about Tabatha and trying to impress her, and all she had to show for it was a lower grade.

1   What do you think is the main message of the passage? How could you use this message in your own life? Use details from the passage in your answer.

In your answer, be sure to
- describe the main message of the passage
- relate the main message to your own life
- use details from the passage
- write an answer of between 1 and 2 pages

Hint

There are two parts to this writing task. You should start by describing what the message of the passage is. This is the lesson that Samantha learns, and also the lesson that readers learn. After describing the message, you should write about how it relates to you. Write a paragraph or two describing how you could use the message to help you in your own life.

One important thing to remember when writing about how the message applies to your life is that you do not have to write about the exact same situation. Think about the general message of the passage rather than what Samantha learns specifically. For example, you might apply the message to your sporting life and write about not being distracted or put off by another team member who is more talented than you.

Planning Page

Summary
Write a brief summary of what you are going to write about.

Supporting Details
Write down the facts, details, or examples you are going to include in your answer.

Outline
Write a plan for what you are going to write. Include the main points you want to cover and the order you will cover them.

Task 4: Personal Narrative Writing Task

Directions: Read the writing prompt below. Use the planning page to plan your writing. Then write or type your answer.

Many people worry about an event coming up and then realize there was nothing to worry about when the event happens. Think of a time when you worried about something a lot and realized it was silly to worry about it later.

Write a personal narrative that describes the situation. Describe what you worried about, what happened, and why there was no need to worry about it.

Hint

When writing compositions like this, think of it as writing a short story where you are the main character. Just like in a short story, the main character has a problem.

In this story, the problem is that you are worrying about something. The start of the story should introduce this problem by telling what you are worrying about.

The middle of the story will tell what happens. You might describe why the problem you were worrying about didn't happen or how things were not as bad as you thought.

The end of the story can describe how you realized there was nothing to worry about in the end. The end can include your final feelings about the situation. You might tell how you felt silly for worrying or how you decided not to worry so much in the future.

Planning Page

Summary
Write a brief summary of what you are going to write about.

Outline
Write a plan for what you are going to write. Include the main points you want to cover and the order you will cover them.

Writing and Editing Checklist

After you finish writing your personal narrative, you can use this guide to review and edit your work. Use the questions as a guide to finding ways you can improve your work.

Writing Checklist

- ✓ Does your work have a strong opening? Does it introduce the main ideas or set the scene well?
- ✓ Is your work well-organized? Is related information grouped together? Does each paragraph have one main idea?
- ✓ Does your work have an effective ending? Does it tie up the events well?
- ✓ Is your work focused? Are there any details that do not fit with your main ideas?
- ✓ Do your ideas flow well? Have you used words and phrases to link ideas well?
- ✓ Have you used strong words? Are there words that could be replaced with better ones?
- ✓ Have you used effective descriptions? Could your descriptions be improved?
- ✓ Have you used sensory details? Could you add more sensory details to help readers imagine the scene?

Editing Checklist

- ✓ Have you used a variety of sentence structures? Are your sentences all written correctly?
- ✓ Is the grammar correct?
- ✓ Are all words spelled correctly? You can check the spelling of any words you are not sure of.
- ✓ Is punctuation used correctly?
- ✓ If dialogue is used, is it punctuated correctly?
- ✓ Are all words capitalized correctly?

Reading and Writing

Practice Set 10

This practice set contains four writing tasks. These are described below.

Task 1: Short Passage with Questions

This task has a short passage followed by questions. Read each question carefully. Then write your answer in the space provided.

You can also practice writing skills by completing the Core Writing Skills Practice exercise.

Task 2: Short Passage with Questions

This task has a short passage followed by questions. Read each question carefully. Then write your answer in the space provided.

You can also practice writing skills by completing the Core Writing Skills Practice exercise.

Task 3: Short Story Writing Task

This task requires you to write a short story. Read the writing prompt, complete the planning page, and then write or type your answer.

Task 4: Argument Writing Task

This final task requires you to write an argument. Read the writing prompt, complete the planning page, and then write or type your answer.

Task 1: Short Passage with Questions

Beach Day

I love going to the beach! There is no better place to go to get away from all your troubles. You can wander along the edge of the ocean and enjoy the feel of your feet sinking into the cool sand. I sometimes stop to watch the rhythm of the waves as they roll in. And if you close your eyes, the sound of the waves breaking on the shore soothes your mind.

Whenever I'm relaxing at the beach, I lay there for hours and let my mind wander. All I need is a big old shady palm tree, a beach towel, and some peace and quiet. It doesn't get much better than that! In fact, there is not a single place in the whole world that I would rather be!

CORE WRITING SKILLS PRACTICE
WRITE A PERSONAL ESSAY

The author describes something that she likes doing. Think of something that you like doing. Answer the questions below. Then write an essay describing what you like doing and why.

What do you like doing?

_____

What do you like about it?

_____

_____

_____

_____

1   Circle the word that you think best describes the day at the beach described in the passage. Then explain why you made that choice.

boring   **relaxing**   **exciting**

_____

_____

_____

_____

_____

2   The narrator states that she likes to "lay there for hours and let my mind wander." What does the phrase "let my mind wander" mean?

_____

_____

_____

_____

_____

Task 2: Short Passage with Questions

A Challenge

Dear Diary,

I've been trying for months now to solve the Rubik's Cube that Dad bought me last year as a birthday present. He knows that collecting odd and zany things is a fun hobby for me. That's one of the reasons I liked it so much.

All you have to do to solve it is get the nine little squares on each side the same color. It sounds simple, but believe me when I tell you that it is not! No matter how many times I turn it here and there, I just can't solve this Rubik's Cube! I've made a pretty pattern out of it, but haven't come close to solving it. I will just have to try again tomorrow.

Bye for now,

Reggie

CORE WRITING SKILLS PRACTICE
WRITE A DIARY ENTRY

Imagine that Reggie finally solves the Rubik's Cube. On the lines below, describe how Reggie would feel that day. Then write a diary entry from Reggie's point of view describing how she finally solved it.

_____

_____

_____

_____

1   How can you tell that Reggie is determined?

Hint   Focus on the information the passage gives about Reggie. Describe the details that suggest that she is a determined person.

_____

_____

_____

_____

_____

2   What does the picture in the passage most help the reader understand? Use details from the passage to support your answer.

_____

_____

_____

_____

_____

_____

3   How do you think Reggie feels about being unable to solve the Rubik's Cube? Use details from the passage in your answer.

Hint   This question is asking you to make an inference about Reggie's feelings. You can make this inference based on what she writes in the diary entry. You can also use how she sounds, such as whether or not she sounds upset about it.

_____

_____

_____

_____

_____

_____

_____

_____

_____

_____

_____

_____

Writing and Editing Checklist

After you finish writing your answer to question 3, you can use this guide to review and edit your work. Use the questions as a guide to finding ways you can improve your work.

Writing Checklist

- ✓ Does your work have a strong opening? Does it introduce the topic and the main ideas?
- ✓ Is your work well-organized? Is related information grouped together? Does each paragraph have one main idea?
- ✓ Have you clearly explained how Reggie feels? Have you used details from the passage to support your claims?
- ✓ Is your work focused? Are there any details that do not fit with your main ideas?
- ✓ Do your ideas flow well? Have you used words and phrases to link ideas well?

Editing Checklist

- ✓ Have you used a variety of sentence structures? Are your sentences all written correctly?
- ✓ Is the grammar correct?
- ✓ Are all words spelled correctly? You can check the spelling of any words you are not sure of.
- ✓ Is punctuation used correctly?
- ✓ If dialogue is used, is it punctuated correctly?
- ✓ Are all words capitalized correctly?

s

Task 3: Short Story Writing Task

Directions: Read the writing prompt below. Use the planning page to plan your writing. Then write or type your answer.

When Karen and Joe's grandfather had asked them to help him clean out the attic, they hadn't expected the day to be very interesting. But what they found that day changed everything.

Write a story about what Karen and Joe found while cleaning out the attic.

Hint

One way to improve your writing is to focus on how you describe things. You can choose words and phrases that make your writing more interesting.

Imagine that you want to describe how dusty the attic was. Instead of just saying it was dusty, you might say that the dust was so thick that Karen wrote her name in it. By describing things in a more interesting way, you will make your story more interesting to the reader.

You can also give specific details that help the reader imagine the scene. These details can describe sounds and smells as well as sights.

Planning Page

The Story
Write a summary of your story.

The Beginning
Describe what is going to happen at the start of your story.

The Middle
Describe what is going to happen in the middle of your story.

The End
Describe what is going to happen at the end of your story.

Task 4: Argument Writing Task

Directions: Read the writing prompt below. Use the planning page to plan your writing. Then write or type your answer.

Read this piece of advice.

> The greatest mistake you can make in life is to be continually fearing you will make one.
>   -Elbert Hubbard

Do you think this is good advice? Explain why or why not.

Hint

Start by thinking about what the advice means. It means that you should not be afraid to make mistakes. Then think about whether you agree. Think about how this advice relates to your life.

The advice can be applied to many areas. A good essay will be focused. Think about how it relates to one area of your life. It could be your studies, your friendships, or your goals. As you plan your writing, focus on this one area. This will help make sure you produce writing that has a clear and focused idea.

Planning Page

Summary
Write a brief summary of your claim.

Supporting Details
Write down the facts, details, or examples you are going to include.

Outline
Write a plan for what you are going to write. Include the main points you want to cover and the order you will cover them.

Writing and Editing Checklist

After you finish writing your argument, you can use this guide to review and edit your work. Use the questions as a guide to finding ways you can improve your work.

Writing Checklist

- ✓ Does your work have one clear claim?
- ✓ Does your work have a strong opening? Does the opening introduce the topic and state the claim?
- ✓ Is your claim supported? Have you used clear reasons to support your claim?
- ✓ Have you used enough evidence? Is your evidence all relevant?
- ✓ Is your work well-organized? Is related information grouped together? Does each paragraph have one main idea?
- ✓ Do your ideas flow well? Have you used words and phrases to link ideas well?
- ✓ Does your work have a strong ending? Does the ending restate the main idea and tie up the argument?

Editing Checklist

- ✓ Have you used a variety of sentence structures? Are your sentences all written correctly?
- ✓ Is the grammar correct?
- ✓ Are all words spelled correctly? You can check the spelling of any words you are not sure of.
- ✓ Is punctuation used correctly?
- ✓ Are all words capitalized correctly?

Answer Key

Developing Common Core Reading and Writing Skills

The state of Massachusetts has adopted the Common Core State Standards. Student learning throughout the year is based on these standards, and all the questions on the state tests assess these standards. All the questions and exercises in this workbook are based on the knowledge and skills described in the Common Core State Standards. While this workbook focuses specifically on the Common Core writing standards, the questions based on passages also assess Common Core reading standards.

Core Skills Practice Exercises

Each short passage in this workbook includes an exercise focused on one key skill described in the Common Core standards. The answer key identifies the core skill covered by each exercise, and describes what to look for in the student's response.

Scoring Constructed-Response Questions

The short passages in this workbook include constructed-response questions, where students provide a written answer to a question. Short questions are scored out of 2 and longer questions are scored out of 4. The answer key gives guidance on how to score these questions. Use the criteria listed as a guide to scoring these questions, and as a guide for giving the student advice on how to improve an answer.

Scoring Writing Tasks

The writing tasks in this workbook are scored based on rubrics that list the features expected of student writing. These features are based on the Common Core standards and are the same criteria used when scoring writing tasks on assessments. The rubrics used for scoring these questions are included in the back of this book. Use the rubric to score these questions, and as a guide for giving the student advice on how to improve an answer.

Practice Set 1

Task 1: Short Passage with Questions (Scorpion and Frog)

Core Writing Skills Practice

Core skill: Draw evidence from literary texts to support analysis, reflection, and research.

Answer: The student should describe how the scorpion tells the frog that he will drown if he stings the frog.

Q1. Give a score of 0, 1, or 2 based on how many correct details are given.
- The details that show that the passage is a fable include that it begins with the phrase "once upon a time," that the characters are animals, that the animals act like humans, and that the passage has a moral or a lesson to teach.

Q2. Give a score of 0, 1, or 2 based on how well the answer meets the criteria listed.
- It should identify that the theme is about being too trusting, about how people cannot help who they are, or about a selfish person being unable to act any other way.

Task 2: Short Passage with Questions (The Exam)

Core Writing Skills Practice

Core skill: Write arguments to support claims with clear reasons and relevant evidence.

Answer: Use the Argument Writing Rubric to review the work and give a score out of 4.

Q1. Give a score of 0, 1, or 2 based on how many correct things are given.
- The ways that Alex tries include asking Kevin for help, having her mother help her study, and getting her teacher to tutor her.

Q2. Give a score of 0, 1, or 2 based on how well the answer meets the criteria listed.
- It should identify that the word "whiz" indicates that Kevin is very good at math.
- It may give a definition of the word "whiz" as it is used in the passage.
- It may explain that someone who is a whiz at something is naturally very good at it.

Task 3: Long Passage with Essay Question

Use the Informative/Explanatory Writing Rubric to review the work and give a score out of 4.

Task 4: Personal Narrative Writing Task

Use the Narrative Writing Rubric to review the work and give a score out of 4.

Practice Set 2

Task 1: Short Passage with Questions (Doyle Brunson)

Core Writing Skills Practice

Core skill: Write informative/explanatory texts to examine a topic and convey ideas, concepts, and information through the selection, organization, and analysis of relevant content.

Answer: Use the Informative/Explanatory Writing Rubric to give a score out of 4.

Q1. Give a score of 0, 1, or 2 based on how many facts and opinions are correctly listed.
- The facts listed could include that he is also known as "Big Poppa" or "Texas Dolly," has been playing cards for over 50 years, was born in 1933, was born in Fisher County, won the World Series of Poker in 1976 and 1977, or that he was holding the same two cards both times that he won.
- The opinions listed could include that he is one of the most respected card players, is easily recognized in his cowboy hat, has achieved many great things, or that his greatest achievement was his pair of World Series of Poker wins.

Q2. Give a score of 0, 1, or 2 based on how many opinions are correctly listed.
- The student should describe how winning two years in a row is rare or special, and how he was holding the same two cards in the final hand of both his winning years.

Task 2: Short Passage with Questions (Food Poisoning)

Core Writing Skills Practice

Core skill: Use common, grade-appropriate Greek or Latin affixes and roots as clues to the meaning of a word.

Answer: unfreeze: to thaw or make something no longer frozen
refreeze: to freeze again
Words that can have *un-* and *re-*prefixes include *do*, *load*, *pack*, *tie*, and *cover*.

Q1. Give a score of 0, 1, or 2 based on how well the answer meets the criteria listed.
- It should explain that food poisoning occurs when the food that people eat contains harmful bacteria.

Q2. Give a score of 0, 1, or 2 based on how well the answer meets the criteria listed.
- It should refer to the bacteria from meat coming into contact with foods that are not cooked before being eaten.

Task 3: Short Story Writing Task

Use the Narrative Writing Rubric to review the work and give a score out of 4.

Task 4: Argument Writing Task

Use the Argument Writing Rubric to review the work and give a score out of 4.

Practice Set 3

Task 1: Short Passage with Questions (Bless You)

Core Writing Skills Practice

Core skill: Conduct short research projects to answer a question, drawing on several sources and refocusing the inquiry when appropriate.

Answer: Reasonable answers could include staying indoors, not playing in grassy areas like parks, wearing sunglasses, keeping windows and doors shut, or taking medication.

Q1. Give a score of 0, 1, or 2 based on how well the answer meets the criteria listed.
- It should identify that the least common cause of sneezing is either in response to light or in response to feeling full.
- It may compare the rare cause with the more common causes of sneezing due to irritation or infection.

Q2. Give a score of 0, 1, or 2 based on how well the answer meets the criteria listed.
- It should identify details from the passage that the student found interesting or surprising.
- It should include a brief explanation of why the details are interesting or surprising.

Task 2: Short Passage with Questions (The Cookie Thief)

Core Writing Skills Practice

Core skill: Write narratives to develop real or imagined experiences or events using effective technique, relevant descriptive details, and well-structured event sequences.

Answer: The student should write a paragraph describing an argument between Max and his sister.

Q1. Give a score of 0, 1, or 2 based on how well the answer meets the criteria listed.
- It should tell how Max remembers eating the cookies when he trips over the container.

Q2. Give a score of 0, 1, or 2 based on how well the answer meets the criteria listed.
- The hyperbole is when Max says that he'll find the thief if it is the last thing he does.
- It should tell how the hyperbole emphasizes Max's strong feelings about finding the thief.

Q3. Give a score of 0, 1, 2, 3, or 4 based on how well the answer meets the criteria listed.
- It may refer to Max's actions in the first paragraph, his dialogue in the second paragraph, the imagery used, the actions described, or the tone of the passage.

Task 3: Long Passage with Essay Question

Use the Informative/Explanatory Writing Rubric to review the work and give a score out of 4.

Task 4: Explanatory Writing Task

Use the Informative/Explanatory Writing Rubric to review the work and give a score out of 4.

Practice Set 4

Task 1: Short Passage with Questions (Nana's Cookie Jar)

Core Writing Skills Practice

Core skill: Write narratives to develop real or imagined experiences or events using effective technique, relevant descriptive details, and well-structured event sequences.

Answer: The student should write a paragraph describing the taste of a cookie. The student should use details and imagery to clearly describe the taste.

Q1. Give a score of 0, 1, or 2 based on how many differences are correctly listed.
- The differences could include that the cookies are soft and chewy, that the choc chips are soft and warm, or that the cookies are nicer.

Q2. Give a score of 0, 1, or 2 based on how well the answer meets the criteria listed.
- It should identify the internal rhyme in the line "They're so chewy and so gooey."
- It should identify the alliteration in the line "Nana's choc chip cookies," "Oh, don't forget the fruity ones," or "and the fresh and fruity jam tarts!"
- It should identify the simile in the line "They're like bursts of sunshine."

Task 2: Short Passage with Questions (Like a Rolling Stone)

Core Writing Skills Practice

Core skill: Conduct short research projects to answer a question, drawing on several sources and refocusing the inquiry when appropriate.

Answer: The student should name a band he or she likes, and research basic information about the band. The student should provide correct answers to the questions listed.

Q1. Give a score of 0, 1, or 2 based on how well the answer meets the criteria listed.
- It should make a reasonable inference about how the author feels about The Rolling Stones. The inference could be that the author likes or admires The Rolling Stones. The inference should be supported by information in the passage.

Q2. Give a score of 0, 1, or 2 based on how many correct details are given.
- The details listed could include that they have been playing since 1962, that they have released over 30 albums, that they have sold over 200 million albums, or that other artists and bands have covered their songs.

Task 3: Argument Writing Task

Use the Argument Writing Rubric to review the work and give a score out of 4.

Task 4: Short Story Writing Task

Use the Narrative Writing Rubric to review the work and give a score out of 4.

Practice Set 5

Task 1: Short Passage with Questions (Amelia Earhart)

Core Writing Skills Practice

Core skill: Write informative/explanatory texts to examine a topic and convey ideas, concepts, and information through the selection, organization, and analysis of relevant content.

Answer: Use the Informative/Explanatory Writing Rubric to give a score out of 4.

Q1. Give a score of 0, 1, or 2 based on how well the answer meets the criteria listed.
- It should explain that Amelia Earhart was a pioneer because she did things that no woman had ever done before.
- It may describe how she was the first woman to fly solo across the Atlantic Ocean, how she set many records, or how female pilots were rare at the time.

Q2. Give a score of 0, 1, or 2 based on how well the answer meets the criteria listed.
- It should explain that the second paragraph describes Amelia's disappearance.
- It may describe the second paragraph's purpose as being to describe a mystery.

Task 2: Short Passage with Questions (Disappearing Dessert)

Core Writing Skills Practice

Core skill: Write narratives to develop real or imagined experiences or events using effective technique, relevant descriptive details, and well-structured event sequences.

Answer: Use the Narrative Writing Rubric to review the work and give a score out of 4.

Q1. Give a score of 0, 1, or 2 based on how well the answer meets the criteria listed.
- The main events should include that Tony keeps meeting people and giving them cannolis, and then has none left and gives his uncle an empty bag.

Q2. Give a score of 0, 1, or 2 based on how well the answer meets the criteria listed.
- It should refer to how Tony accidentally gives all the cannolis away, and how Uncle Benny opens the bag and finds nothing inside.

Q3. Give a score of 0, 1, 2, 3, or 4 based on how well the answer meets the criteria listed.
- It should explain that Tony had cannolis in the bag, but gave cannolis to everyone he met on his way to the barber shop.

Task 3: Long Passage with Essay Question

Use the Informative/Explanatory Writing Rubric to review the work and give a score out of 4.

Task 4: Explanatory Writing Task

Use the Informative/Explanatory Writing Rubric to review the work and give a score out of 4.

Practice Set 6

Task 1: Short Passage with Questions (Nintendo)

Core Writing Skills Practice

Core skill: Draw evidence from informational texts to support analysis, reflection, and research.

Answer: The student should describe how Nintendo eventually became successful.

Q1. Give a score of 0, 1, or 2 based on how many correct examples are given.
- The early businesses include making playing cards, a taxi company, a television network, and a food company.

Q2. Give a score of 0, 1, or 2 based on how well the answer meets the criteria listed.
- It should list the entertainment products released by Nintendo in order from the earliest product to the most recent product.
- The products released in order from earliest to latest are: Nintendo Entertainment System (1983); Game Boy (1989); Nintendo DS (2004); and Nintendo Wii (2006).

Task 2: Short Passage with Questions (The Fox and the Hound)

Core Writing Skills Practice

Core skill: Draw evidence from informational texts to support analysis, reflection, and research.

Answer: The student should write the correct event next to each year on the timeline.

Q1. Give a score of 0, 1, or 2 based on how many facts and opinions are correctly listed.
- The facts listed could include that *The Fox and the Hound* was written by Daniel P. Mannix and first published in 1967, that the film *The Fox and the Hound* was the most expensive animated film ever made, that the film was released in 1981, or that *The Fox and the Hound 2* was released in 2006.
- The opinions listed could include that the film was very successful, that *The Fox and the Hound 2* was not as successful, or that *The Fox and the Hound 2* was enchanting and entertaining.

Q2. Give a score of 0, 1, or 2 based on how well the answer meets the criteria listed.
- It should give reasonable examples of how the statement could be supported, such as by including information on the amount of people who saw the film, giving facts on the profits made, or describing the awards won by the first film.

Task 3: Short Story Writing Task

Use the Narrative Writing Rubric to review the work and give a score out of 4.

Task 4: Argument Writing Task

Use the Argument Writing Rubric to review the work and give a score out of 4.

Practice Set 7

Task 1: Short Passage with Questions (Tau Ceti)

Core Writing Skills Practice

Core skill: Determine the meaning of words and phrases as they are used in a text, including figurative, connotative, and technical meanings.

Answer: The student should write a valid definition of each term. Examples are given below.
constellation: a group of stars that form a set pattern
spectral type: a way of classifying stars based on their color
light year: the distance that light travels in one year

Q1. Give a score of 0, 1, or 2 based on how well the answer meets the criteria listed.
- Similarities include that they are both large stars, have a similar mass, have the same spectral type, and can both be seen with the naked eye.
- Differences include that Tau Ceti is farther from Earth and has more debris.

Q2. Give a score of 0, 1, or 2 based on how well the answer meets the criteria listed.
- It should make a valid supported prediction about the impact of Jane Greaves' findings, such as that her findings changed the belief that Tau Ceti could be home to life.

Task 2: Short Passage with Questions (The Highest Price)

Core Writing Skills Practice

Core skill: Write narratives to develop real or imagined experiences or events using effective technique, relevant descriptive details, and well-structured event sequences.

Answer: Use the Narrative Writing Rubric to review the work and give a score out of 4.

Q1. Give a score of 0, 1, or 2 based on how well the answer meets the criteria listed.
- It should use relevant details from the passage such as how Captain Ludikar is worried about his people, how he seems to care more about his people than himself, or how he gets little sleep because he is worried about his people.

Q2. Give a score of 0, 1, or 2 based on how well the answer meets the criteria listed.
- It should identify the genre as science fiction.
- The evidence could be specific, such as stating that the passage involves space travel and visiting another planet. The evidence could be general, such as stating that the passage involves things that are not possible now and that it involves science.

Task 3: Long Passage with Essay Question

Use the Narrative Writing Rubric to review the work and give a score out of 4.

Task 4: Explanatory Writing Task

Use the Informative/Explanatory Writing Rubric to review the work and give a score out of 4.

Practice Set 8

Task 1: Short Passage with Questions (Michelangelo)

Core Writing Skills Practice

Core skill: Draw evidence from informational texts to support analysis, reflection, and research.

Answer: It should describe how you can tell that the author admires Michelangelo. It could refer to details given about him, words used to describe him, or the positive tone.

Q1. Give a score of 0, 1, or 2 based on how well the answer meets the criteria listed.
- It should describe why Michelangelo can be considered a "typical Renaissance man."
- It may describe how a Renaissance man was someone with talents in many areas.
- It should refer to how Michelangelo was an artist, a sculptor, a poet, an engineer, and an architect.

Q2. Give a score of 0, 1, or 2 based on how well the answer meets the criteria listed.
- It should explain that the statue was too large and heavy to be placed on the roof.
- It should describe how the statue could not be lifted up to the roof, and may describe how machinery was not available at the time.

Task 2: Short Passage with Questions (A Helping Hand)

Core Writing Skills Practice

Core skill: Write arguments to support claims with clear reasons and relevant evidence.

Answer: Use the Argument Writing Rubric to review the work and give a score out of 4.

Q1. Give a score of 0, 1, or 2 based on how well the answer meets the criteria listed.
- It should give an opinion on whether or not Dr. Price is an inspirational person.
- It should include a fully-supported explanation of why or why not.

Q2. Give a score of 0, 1, or 2 based on how well the answer meets the criteria listed.
- It should circle one of the words. Either word is acceptable, as long as it is supported.
- It should include a well-supported explanation of why the student chose that word.

Q3. Give a score of 0, 1, 2, 3, or 4 based on how well the answer meets the criteria listed.
- It should draw a valid conclusion about what people can learn from Dr. Price.
- It may include a personal response on what the student learned from Dr. Price.

Task 3: Argument Writing Task

Use the Argument Writing Rubric to review the work and give a score out of 4.

Task 4: Short Story Writing Task

Use the Narrative Writing Rubric to review the work and give a score out of 4.

Practice Set 9

Task 1: Short Passage with Questions (Constantinople)

Core Writing Skills Practice
Core skill: Draw evidence from informational texts to support analysis, reflection, and research.
Answer: It should refer to how the Byzantine Empire had seemed unstoppable or to how the Fall of Constantinople was the end of the Byzantine Empire.

Q1. Give a score of 0, 1, or 2 based on how well the answer meets the criteria listed.
- It should explain that the Fall of Constantinople refers to when the city was captured by the Ottomans, and that this was the end of the Byzantine Empire.

Q2. Give a score of 0, 1, or 2 based on how many correct changes are listed.
- The changes include that Emperor Constantine XI was no longer the area's ruler, that Constantinople became the capital of the Ottoman Empire, and that the Byzantine Empire no longer existed.

Task 2: Short Passage with Questions (Poor King Henri)

Core Writing Skills Practice
Core skill: Draw evidence from literary texts to support analysis, reflection, and research.
Answer: The student should give an opinion on whether the simile explains King Henri's change of mood well. The student may explain that the simile shows a sudden and positive mood change, and may also refer to how King Henri's moods are also related to the seasons.

Q1. Give a score of 0, 1, or 2 based on how well the answer meets the criteria listed.
- It should explain that King Henri's bad mood caused his friends to start avoiding him, which made him focus even more on his aching joints.

Q2. Give a score of 0, 1, or 2 based on how well the answer meets the criteria listed.
- It should give an opinion on whether or not the celebration made up for King Henri's poor behavior.
- It should include a reasonable and well-supported explanation of why the student has that opinion.

Task 3: Long Passage with Essay Question

Use the Informative/Explanatory Writing Rubric to review the work and give a score out of 4.

Task 4: Personal Narrative Writing Task

Use the Narrative Writing Rubric to review the work and give a score out of 4.

Practice Set 10

Task 1: Short Passage with Questions (Beach Day)

Core Writing Skills Practice

Core skill: Write informative/explanatory texts to examine a topic and convey ideas, concepts, and information through the selection, organization, and analysis of relevant content.

Answer: Use the Informative/Explanatory Writing Rubric to give a score out of 4.

Q1. Give a score of 0, 1, or 2 based on how well the answer meets the criteria listed.
- It should circle one of the words. Any of the words could be reasonable answers, as long as the choice is supported.
- It should include a reasonable and well-supported explanation for the word chosen.

Q2. Give a score of 0, 1, or 2 based on how well the answer meets the criteria listed.
- It should explain the meaning of the phrase "let my mind wander."
- It should explain that the phrase means that she was relaxing and thinking about things.

Task 2: Short Passage with Questions (A Challenge)

Core Writing Skills Practice

Core skill: Write narratives to develop real or imagined experiences or events using effective technique, relevant descriptive details, and well-structured event sequences.

Answer: Use the Narrative Writing Rubric to review the work and give a score out of 4.

Q1. Give a score of 0, 1, or 2 based on how well the answer meets the criteria listed.
- It should explain that you can tell that Reggie is determined because she has not given up on trying to solve the Rubik's Cube and keeps trying.

Q2. Give a score of 0, 1, or 2 based on how well the answer meets the criteria listed.
- It may explain that the picture shows that the Rubik's Cube has different colored squares, and that the picture shows how you can twist and move the squares.

Q3. Give a score of 0, 1, 2, 3, or 4 based on how well the answer meets the criteria listed.
- It should make a reasonable inference about how Reggie feels about being unable to solve the Rubik's Cube.
- The inference could be that Reggie feels challenged, frustrated, or determined.

Task 3: Short Story Writing Task

Use the Narrative Writing Rubric to review the work and give a score out of 4.

Task 4: Argument Writing Task

Use the Argument Writing Rubric to review the work and give a score out of 4.

INFORMATIVE/EXPLANATORY WRITING RUBRIC

This writing rubric is based on the Common Core standards and describes the features that are expected in student writing. Give students a score out of 4 based on how well the answer meets the criteria. Then average the scores to give a total score out of 4. Students can also be given feedback and guidance based on the criteria below.

	Score	Notes
Organization and Purpose To receive a full score, the response will: • have an opening that introduces the topic • have a clear focus • be well-organized with related information grouped together • use formatting (e.g. headings) and graphics (e.g. charts, diagrams) when appropriate • provide a concluding statement or section		
Evidence and Elaboration To receive a full score, the response will: • develop the topic with facts, details, quotations, or examples • include relevant text-based evidence when appropriate		
Written Expression To receive a full score, the response will: • be clear and easy to understand • have good transitions between ideas • use language to communicate ideas effectively • have an appropriate style		
Writing Conventions To receive a full score, the response will: • have few or no spelling errors • have few or no grammar errors • have few or no capitalization errors • have few or no punctuation errors		
Total Score		

ARGUMENT WRITING RUBRIC

This writing rubric is based on the Common Core standards and describes the features that are expected in student writing. Give students a score out of 4 based on how well the answer meets the criteria. Then average the scores to give a total score out of 4. Students can also be given feedback and guidance based on the criteria below.

	Score	Notes
Organization and Purpose To receive a full score, the response will: • have an opening that introduces the topic and states the claim • have a clear focus • be well-organized with related information grouped together • provide a concluding statement or section		
Evidence and Elaboration To receive a full score, the response will: • express clear reasons to support the claim • include evidence to support the claim • include relevant text-based evidence when appropriate		
Written Expression To receive a full score, the response will: • be clear and easy to understand • have good transitions between ideas • use language to communicate ideas effectively • have an appropriate style		
Writing Conventions To receive a full score, the response will: • have few or no spelling errors • have few or no grammar errors • have few or no capitalization errors • have few or no punctuation errors		
Total Score		

NARRATIVE WRITING RUBRIC

This writing rubric is based on the Common Core standards and describes the features that are expected in student writing. Give students a score out of 4 based on how well the answer meets the criteria. Then average the scores to give a total score out of 4. Students can also be given feedback and guidance based on the criteria below.

	Score	Notes
Organization and Purpose To receive a full score, the response will: • have an effective opening that introduces the situation, characters, or event • have a logical and organized event sequence • have an effective ending		
Development and Elaboration To receive a full score, the response will: • have clearly developed characters, setting, and events • use narrative techniques such as dialogue and pacing effectively • use precise words and phrases • use relevant descriptive details • use sensory language		
Written Expression To receive a full score, the response will: • be clear and easy to understand • have good transitions between ideas • use language to communicate ideas effectively		
Writing Conventions To receive a full score, the response will: • have few or no spelling errors • have few or no grammar errors • have few or no capitalization errors • have few or no punctuation errors		
Total Score		

Made in the USA
Middletown, DE
10 January 2016